Capitalist Theology

Written by William Bethea

Published by

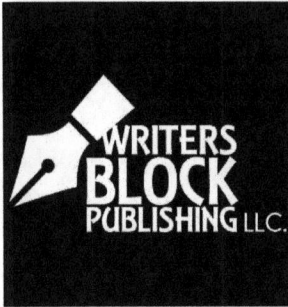

www.writersblockpublishingllc.com

Index

Introduction

Two Thousand years ago, in the barn of a roadside inn, the most consequential child was born. In only 33 years of life, that child managed to turn both the religious and secular worlds on their heads. Regardless of one's opinion concerning his message or declaration of divinity, It's hard to argue that any person in recorded history has had a great or long-lasting impact as Jesus of Nazareth. Yet, here we are still at the dawn of a new millennium and the Church, the institutional legacy of Christ, finds itself faced with a crisis, which is, in my opinion, of its own making. That crisis is irrelevance in the modern age.

As society becomes more secularly bent, the number of believers in this country and abroad continues to shrink. [1]Churches are closing their doors, clergy and laity alike are abandoning the faith, but perhaps worst of all is the possibility few outside of the church seem to care. [2]Some have even argued this is a good thing. Religion after all is the opiate of the masses.

Those of us who are Believers would argue to the contrary. Christ declared that we, his disciples, are the salt of the earth.

---

[1] Frank Newport, "In U.S., Four in 10 Report Attending Church in Last Week," Gallup.com (Gallup, January 6, 2020), https://news.gallup.com/poll/166613/four-report-attending-churchlast-week.aspx)

[2] David Kinnaman and Roxanne Stone, "Americans Divided on the Importance of Church," Barna Group (Barna Group Inc, March 24, 2014), https://www.barna.com/research/americans-divided-on-theimportance-of-church/)

However, when Christ made that declaration, he did so, acknowledging,
"...if the salt have lost his savor, wherewith shall it be salted? it is thenceforth good for nothing, but to be cast out, and to be trodden under foot of men." (Matthew 5:13 KJV)

The greatest failure of the 20th and 21st-Century Church is our loss of identity, our purpose for existing as an organized body. Yes, our great commission is to go out into the four corners of the world sharing the gospel of Christ Jesus, but as the old riddle says, "if a tree falls in the woods and no one is around to hear, does it make a sound?" We have a message of hope, and salvation to share with the world, but what purpose does that message serve if no one cares to listen?

Today believers find themselves in a state described by one of the greatest "social justice warriors" of the 20th century when he wrote, "The contemporary church is so often a weak, ineffectual voice with an uncertain sound."[3] We have willfully ignored, if not sanctioned, the evils of society while, ironically enough, adopting its systems, creating a Frankenstein's monster I call Capitalist Theology. We have become, in many ways, a reflection of the worst aspects of contemporary society. The modern Church is a self-interested, and at times self-serving institution which infects its members with the same mentality. This mentality has led the Church and its people to become indifferent and irrelevant to a good portion of the world.

I am not ashamed to say that my greatest fear is living an inconsequential life. Therefore, the idea of dedicating the

---

[3] Martin L King, ed. Ali B Ali-Dinar, Letter from a Birmingham Jail [King, Jr.] (University of Pennsylvania), accessed April 14, 2020, https://www.africa.upenn.edu/Articles_Gen/Letter_Birmingham.html)

majority of my years to an institution that is in the state I described above has become unacceptable to me. So I find myself with two choices, each with its own harrowing consequences. Should I abandon the institution entirely or become the change I desire to see? This book is not a declaration of the Church's demise, but hopefully, it serves as both an alarm and a call to action.

There will be those who chafe at this book's content. I won't apologize for making you do so. There will be those who dismiss it entirely. I won't concern myself with that either. My goal is not to be provocative, but it is to provoke the saints of God to action. My prayer and my hope is for the institution we call the Church to return to relevance. This begins with bringing light to the issues that have caused such a state.

I will be arguing the following points.

1. The Institutional Church, as well as its members, has developed and practices a philosophy of self-interestedness.
2. This philosophy has caused the institution and its members to ignore both its corrupted state and that of secular institutions.
3. This pattern of neglect caused the Church to become irrelevant to much of society that suffers at the hands of secular institutions.
4. This state of irrelevance has caused the Church's message of hope and salvation to be ignored by much of society.
5. The Church will return to relevance when it abandons its philosophy of self-interestedness and follows God's plan of service to him through service to others.

In addition, I will argue how the philosophy of self-interestedness can be abandoned, and the Church can return to relevance via the following:

1. The institution's authority and that of its leaders cannot go unchecked by those over whom that authority is exercised.
2. The laity must develop capacity and desire for critical thinking and spiritual self-sufficiency to make the first point possible.
3. Both the institution and the people must abandon secular models of operation that encourage self-interestedness in the Church.
4. Both the institution and its members must commit to doing God's will through selfless service to each other.
5. Both the institution and its members must commit to serving the world through holistic ministry.

In addition to the previous objective, I will be putting forth a concept I mentioned earlier that I believe most accurately describes the theology of the contemporary institutional Church, that being Capitalist Theology. To summarize, Capitalist Theology is a religious belief system characterized by the adoption, and therefore the promotion of capitalist sensibilities and principles. Bodies that practice Capitalist Theology exhibit any number, if not all these characteristics:

1. Reliance upon and manipulating the governed's desire for material consumption through faith in the system, as both a means of pacification of the governed and perpetuation.

2. Emphasizes and incentives self-interestedness over service
3. The concentration of power in a few individuals or groups within the governing body.
4. Legitimizes concentration of power and dissipates opposition through scriptural manipulation and cronyism

As you can see, Capitalist Theology shares many similarities with advanced secular Capitalism. This is not a coincidence, but a direct result of the Church's failure to resist conforming to and adopting the world's economic and social system.

Please understand, this book should not be read as a condemnation of the institutional Church. Rather, it is both a diagnosis of what ails it and recommendation for treatment. Do I believe this book is a definitive answer to the Church's relevance problem? No. Such a thing can only be resolved when the entire body of believers is working together. However, I do not assume that gives me or any other saint permission to stand idly by and wait for a solution to fall from heaven, pun intended.

> "Even so faith, if it hath not works, is dead, being alone. Yea, a man may say, Thou hast faith, and I have works: shew me thy faith without thy works, and I will shew thee my faith by my works. Was not Abraham our father justified by works, when he had offered Isaac his son upon the altar? Seest thou how faith wrought with his works, and by works was faith made perfect? And the scripture was fulfilled which saith, Abraham believed God, and it was imputed unto him for righteousness: and he was called the Friend of God. Ye see then how that by works a man is justified, and not by faith only. Likewise also was not Rahab the harlot justified by works, when she had received the messengers, and had sent them out another way? For as the body without the Spirit is dead, so faith without works is dead also." (James 2:17-18, 21-26 KJV)

I want to end this introduction by telling a story. My mother, the seventh of ten children, along with two of her sisters, made it their purpose to make disciples out of their other siblings. After years of imploring, my mother and her older sister finally convinced my youngest uncle to join them at a prayer meeting. I was not there, but my mother came home full of joy and emotion. I knew before she even told me, my uncle had given his life to Christ. No more than a year or two later, he was murdered in cold blood. Despite the rumors and the gossip bring spread, he was not a thug.

He was not a gang member or a criminal, nor did he associate with any. He was a family man, a quiet man, a working man. He did not deserve what happened to him. I had stopped going to church with my mother, and this tragedy gave me all the more reasons to stay away. I remember I was angry, confused, and frustrated, but my mother was strangely at peace despite the tragedy and all the drama that ensued. My mother said to me one day without being provoked,

"William, I was angry with the Lord for longer than I should've been, and I needed to repent."

I said to her, "You have a right to be angry. I can't understand why God would allow such a thing to happen to a good person".

My mother said to me, "I believe God took Marc, because there was nothing left here for him."

It took me a very long time to understand what she was saying. When I did, I became convinced that nothing happens without God's permission, and therefore nothing happens by chance. I don't believe it is God's will for evil to persists, but I believe God gives us the agency to determine how much evil will be perpetuated by us to each other. Every human being is born with a purpose. As long as a person is in this world, there is an assignment to be completed.

When the Church was born in that upper room somewhere in Jerusalem 2000 years ago, it was not by chance. The Spirit of God empowered the saints on purpose and for a reason. That reason was not to bemoan the state of both the Church and society, then lock ourselves in our churches cut off from the groaning of God's creation. At the same time, we indulged our self-interested tendencies praying God would compel someone else to do the work we had been commissioned to. That reason was not to make kings of clergymen or saints into serfs. That reason was not to be the opiate of the masses but the cure for hopelessness.

 The Church may be sick, but it is not dead, and as long as there are two or three believers left in this world, its mission will still be active. Christ gave us the commission to be the light of the world, to allow men to see our good works and give him glory. The light may be hidden by a bushel called self-interestedness, but my hope is we can remove that bushel, cast it aside, and return the light to its proper place. My prayer is that this book will help do that.

On the Importance of Relevance

Considering this book revolves around the theme of relevance, I think we must first answer two questions. What is relevance, and why is it important. I say this because there are saints who will argue that relevance is irrelevant to the Church. A common refrain among saints is "We are in this world but not of it". It has become so common, in fact many of us quote it as scripture (it is not I checked).

 The Bible does instruct us to "be not conformed to this world but be ye transformed by the renewing of your minds" (Rom 13:1 KJV). It goes on further to say, "Do not love the world [of sin that opposes God and His precepts], nor the things that are in the world. If anyone loves the world, the love of the Father is not in him." (1 John 2:15 AMP). Christ gives these instructions concerning our great commission to spread his gospel:

"Whoever does not welcome you, nor listen to your message, as you leave that house or city, shake the dust [of it] off your feet [in contempt, breaking all ties]. I assure you and most solemnly say to you, it will be more tolerable on the day of judgment for the land of Sodom and Gomorrah than for that city [since it rejected the Messiah's messenger]." (Matt 10:14-15 AMP)

So, the question is, should we even care whether we are received by society or not? I would answer that question with another. What was the purpose of Christ's commission if not the salvation of the world, more specifically the people living in it? Was it just to keep us busy until his return? Obviously, the answer is no:

"The Lord does not delay [as though He were unable to act] and is not slow about His promise, as some count slowness, but is [extraordinarily] patient toward you, not wishing for any to perish but for all to come to repentance." (2 Peter 3:9 AMP) When Christ died, he did so for the entirety of humanity, believers, and non-believers alike. I'm sure everyone reading knows this because, as the most well-known passage in the Bible states, "For God so loved the world that he gave his only begotten Son..." (John 3:16 KJV). This tells us Christ died not out of obligation but for the love of humanity. As we'll discuss later, part of salvation is the spirit baptism or God's Spirit coming and dwelling inside the heart of a believer.

Now with the Spirit of God comes God's love for humanity. Therefore, if we have God in us, we ought to have love for all of God's children, believers, and non. In fact, the Bible states that anyone who claims to have the Spirit of God, but no love for his neighbor is a liar (1 John 4:12).
Furthermore, the Apostle Paul says this concerning love:

> "If I speak with the tongues of men and of angels, but have not love [for others growing out of God's love for me], then I have become only a noisy gong or a clanging cymbal [just an annoying distraction]. And if I have the gift of prophecy [and speak a new message from God to the people], and understand all mysteries, and [possess] all knowledge; and if I have all [sufficient] faith so that I can remove mountains, but do not have love [reaching out to others], I am nothing. If I give all my possessions to feed the poor, and if I surrender my body to be burned, but do not have love, it does me no good at all." (1 Cor 13:1-3 AMP)

We can conclude then that Christians ought not to fall in love with the systems, the concepts, the mores, or the world's interests. The world's people, on the other hand, are a different story.

"You are the light of [Christ to] the world. A city set on a hill cannot be hidden; nor does anyone light a lamp and put it under a basket, but on a lampstand, and it gives light to all who are in the house. Let your light shine before men in such a way that they may see your good deeds and moral excellence, and [recognize and honor and] glorify your Father who is in heaven." (Matt 5:14-16 AMP)

Now, this begs the question, if you love someone and you see that person in trouble, would it not compel you to get them out of that trouble? Therefore, we, as Christians, should feel compelled by love to help a troubled world through both our witness and service. However, if the object of your advances has no interest in you or your advances, what reason do they have to entertain anything you may have to say? Or perhaps more familiar is the analogy of the tree that falls with no one present to hear or see it do so. Does it even make a sound?

 Therefore relevance is important. The relevance I'm speaking of is simply what matters, what has cultural or societal value. I don't believe Christians should concern themselves with relevance as it pertains to popular culture. This is where distinguishing between the cares of the world and society itself becomes important.

Many Christians are adapting themselves and their practices to be palatable for popular culture. We call it "keeping up with the times" and "progressive ministry." Many churches have traded organs for guitars and keyboards, suits and skirts for tee shirts and skinny jeans, Bibles and notepads for tablets and cell phones, which is not a bad thing. I want to make that explicitly clear; there is nothing wrong or "sinful" about modernization as long as salvation remains the primary message.

Unfortunately, many contemporary and traditional churches are adapting their message to appeal to secular i.e. capitalistic interests. Salvation is no longer the central focus of many ministries. Instead, it has become financial prosperity, marital success, physical and mental wellness, and so on. Once again, none of these things are inherently "bad". As I've already said, a holistic approach to ministry is one of the keys to maintaining relevance. The problem arises when secular interests become the primary, if not the sole purpose, of a ministry. This focus on secular interests creates a secularized church that is arguably not even a church any longer.

It creates a church in which preachers are little more than glorified motivational speakers. It creates a church in which worship leaders are little more than performers. It creates a church that is no longer a church, but an inspirational social club.

It's important for the Church to not completely neglect secular needs. However, it is just as important for a church to prioritize salvation and the preservation thereof, above all other objectives. I cannot stress this fact enough. I am personally offended by churches who make spiritual salvation and wellness an afterthought of their ministry in favor of material wellness. "For what profit is it to a man if he gains the whole world, and loses his own soul? Or what will a man give in exchange for his soul? (Matt 16:26 NKJV).

Suffice to say relevance is more than relatability, although that helps. A consistent display of societal impact establishes an institution's relevance. What tangible impact does an institution make on the society in which it exists? How much of an impact, positive or negative, would an institution's demise have on society? How much does society do to preserve or destroy an institution? These are the questions that need to be asked in order to determine relevance. Now, most Christians would argue that the demise of the Church would be catastrophic to society, but is that what society believes? There are times, this being one, when perception is just as if not more important than reality.

I want you to take note of this Barna Group survey's troubling results: "…people offered a variety of answers [to what helps them grow in faith] prayer, family or friends, reading the Bible, having children—but the Church did not even crack the top-10 list. "[4]Although church involvement was once a cornerstone of American life, U.S. adults today are evenly divided on the importance of attending church. While half (49%) say it is "somewhat" or "very" important, the other 51% say it is "not too" or "not at all" important."[5]

Based on this survey, I have drawn the following conclusion. The majority of people have not stopped coming to church, because they want a more secularized message, which makes sense. Considering many of our ministries have already turned to secularization and yet are continuing to wax older and wane smaller, but because they believe the Church is incapable of fulfilling their spiritual needs. Could it be that the Church has become more secularly focused than society? Therefore, the

---

[4] David Kinnaman and Roxanne Stone, "Americans Divided on the Importance of Church," Barna Group (Barna Group Inc, March 24, 2014), https://www.barna.com/research/americans-divided-on-theimportance-of-church/)
[5] David Kinnaman and Roxanne Stone, "Americans Divided on the Importance of Church," Barna Group (Barna Group Inc, March 24, 2014), https://www.barna.com/research/americans-divided-on-theimportance-of-church/)

answer to the relevance problem is not a more secularized message or ministry.

As we draw to the end of this chapter, I want to put forth a theory. From the 1930s up to today, Gallup has asked Americans every week to report whether they had attended a religious service or not in the past seven days. When researching for this book, I expected to see a steady decline over that span of time, but surprisingly attendance was at its lowest point in 1939 at 37%.[6] It wasn't until the 1950s that we saw a spike in attendance to 49% of Americans each week.[7] What's interesting is that though attendance was low throughout the Depression and WWII years, most Americans were more likely to say religion was a "very important" part of their lives (75%) than at any other point in the last 74 years.[8]

The number of Americans to respond as such steadily decreased from the 1930s until the late 1970s to about half of Americans (it has hovered near that mark, with a few exceptions).[9] So why the sudden uptick in attendance? Though

[6] Frank Newport, "In U.S., Four in 10 Report Attending Church in Last Week," Gallup.com (Gallup, January 6, 2020), https://news.gallup.com/poll/166613/four-report-attending-churchlast-week.aspx)

[7] Carol Tucker, "The 1950s – Powerful Years for Religion," USC News (University of Southern California, April 3, 2012), https://news.usc.edu/25835/The-1950s-Powerful-Years-for-Religion/)

[8] Frank Newport, "In U.S., Four in 10 Report Attending Church in Last Week," Gallup.com (Gallup, January 6, 2020), https://news.gallup.com/poll/166613/four-report-attending-churchlast-week.aspx)

[9] Frank Newport, "In U.S., Four in 10 Report Attending Church in Last Week," Gallup.com (Gallup, January 6, 2020), https://news.gallup.com/poll/166613/four-report-attending-churchlast-week.aspx)

the point is debatable, many historians have posited that a desire for normalcy after WWII spurred an emphasis on traditional family values. And what better foundation for family than church? Consider this quote from author Robert Ellwood:

> "'Religion flourished in the '50s for several reasons, partly because of the ever-expanding spiritual marketplace...There were a lot of different options available that would appeal to different kinds of people. Before the war, organized religion was much more restricted'"[10]

So, we can conclude that the reasons behind high attendance rates were just as practical as they were spiritual. Families found what many church seekers today are in search of when on the prowl for a church home, the right fit. Instead of forcing themselves to adapt to the propriety of traditional congregations, folks chose instead to seek out centers of worship that fit them, where they were free to be themselves.

So, we've answered the question of why church attendance spiked in the 50s. We've concluded that it was less a spiritual revival, than a product of convenience. This does not, however, address the steady decline of church attendance following the 50s. I would like for you to consider for a moment the American Church's complacency and even complicity in perpetuating systemic injustice.

During the Civil Rights Era, the response of the Church at large was tepid at best with most remaining silent and, in some cases, vocal in their denouncement of the Civil Rights movement and

---

[10] Carol Tucker, "The 1950s – Powerful Years for Religion," USC News (University of Southern California, April 3, 2012), https://news.usc.edu/25835/The-1950s-Powerful-Years-for-Religion/)

its leaders.[11] Because of revisionist history, and the almost mythic legacy of people like Dr. King magnified by his untimely death, we assume most Christians, or at least Black Christians, stood united for the cause of civil rights; however, the truth is a bit more complicated:

> "There's a growing consensus that justice must be on the black church's agenda, which was not the case even in the old days...Clergymen like King, [Ralph] Abernathy and Adam Clayton Powell had split from conservative [clergy] leaders who distanced themselves from the movement. As a result, their names -- Dr. King's most prominently--became synonymous with the Civil Rights movement, although, in reality, pastors only made up a small sect of leaders and organizers."[12]

The tension between conservative and progressive church leaders, including King within the National Baptist Convention, boiled to the point of a schism and literal fistfight. The progressive leaders broke off and formed the Progressive National Baptist Convention in 1961. While the conservative faction remained and still remains the largest organization of black Baptist Churches.[13] We can infer by this that the majority of the clergy during this time were conservative and found it in their interests not to ally with King or his like-minded fellow clergy.

---

[11] "Public Statement by Eight Alabama Clergymen," M.L.King: 1963 Public statement by 8 Alabama clergymen, accessed April 14, 2020, https://www.massresistance.org/docs/gen/09a/mlk_day/statement.html)

[12] Danielle Cadet, "Black Church's Civil Rights Movement Legacy Is Both A Blessing And A Curse," HuffPost (HuffPost, August 25, 2013), https://www.huffpost.com/entry/black-church-civil-rightsmovement_n_3810530)

[13] Taylor Branch, *Parting the Waters: America in the King Years, 1954-(New York: Simon and Schuster Paperbacks, 2006).*

Truth be told, the Church, often, had a passively antagonistic relationship with the Civil Rights movement
[14] Why? Well, the argument can be and has been made that many black clergy, and parishioners, for that matter, were deterred by the backlash of violent retaliation the movement was causing. One could argue that many traditionalists followed a literal interpretation of particular passages of scripture concerning obeisance to government.

One could also argue that many white clergymen were too afraid of angering their white parishioners by supporting a movement that threatened the status quo, which maintained the balance of power in favor of whites.[15] Whatever the argument, it is hard for me not to draw a correlation between the decline in the public's attendance and perception of the Church and its failure to fully and unequivocally support a just cause. I believe the Church has too often found, and continues to find itself on the sideline, or worse the wrong side of history in terms of social justice.[16]

Now If you're coming of age in the 50s, 60s, even the 70s and you hear these Christians wax on about living, doing, and loving

---

[14] Justin Taylor, "A Conversation with Four Historians on the Response of White Evangelicals to the Civil Rights Movement," The Gospel Coalition, July 1, 2016,
https://www.thegospelcoalition.org/blogs/evangelical-history/aconver sation-with-four-historians-on-the-response-of-whiteevangelicals-to-th e-civil-rights-movement/)
[15] Justin Taylor, "A Conversation with Four Historians on the Response of White Evangelicals to the Civil Rights Movement," The Gospel Coalition, July 1, 2016,
[16] John Eligon, "Where Today's Black Church Leaders Stand on Activism," The New York Times (The New York Times, April 3, 2018), https://www.nytimes.com/2018/04/03/us/mlk-church-civilrights.html ?searchResultPosition=1)

as Christ would, but what you observe is secular folks combating institutional immorality and wickedness while the Church remains silently, and even in some cases, vocally complicit in the perpetuation of institutional wickedness while continuing to insist on individual moralism, what conclusion would you draw about the Church?

Furthermore, why should you care about an institution that doesn't seem to care about you or the society in which it exists? I believe this led an entire generation to conclude the Church was either out of touch with, or apathetic to the evils of the natural world. It caused that generation to conclude that the Church was more interested in shallow moralism than true justice or righteousness and thus was hypocritical and socially irrelevant. According to Joanne Beckmann of Duke University, this is a likely reason why the Church has been dismissed:

> "The Church, along with government, big business, and the military—those composing "the Establishment"—was denounced by the young adults of the '60s for its materialism, power ploys, self-interest, and smug complacency."[17]

All of this is not to say overnight the church emptied its pews, as research shows us majority of Baby Boomers remained faithful to traditional beliefs.[18] What did happen is the

---

[17] Beckman, Joanne. "Religion in Post-World War II America." *Religion in Post-World War II America, Twentieth Century, Divining America: Religion in American History, TeacherServe, National Humanities Center*, Duke University , Oct. 2000, nationalhumanitiescenter.org/tserve/twenty/tkeyinfo/trelww2.htm.
[18] Beckman, Joanne. "Religion in Post-World War II America." *Religion in Post-World War II America, Twentieth Century, Divining America: Religion in American History, TeacherServe, National Humanities*

floodgates were opened for doubt. In this era, those raised Christian saw reason to demur their beliefs and more importantly the institution that taught them those beliefs.

Consequently, those Baby Boomers became more open to alternative avenues of truth and spirituality. That open-mindedness was passed down to their children and so on. NYU sociology professor Michael Hout supports this claim:

> "Many Millennials have parents who are Baby Boomers and Boomers expressed to their children that it's important to think for themselves – that they find their own moral compass. Also, they rejected the idea that a good kid is an obedient kid. That's at odds with organizations, like churches, that have a long tradition of official teaching and obedience"[19]

The numbers seem to support this claim as only 46% of Millennials self-identify as Christian and 41% claim no religious affiliation.[20]

Center, Duke University , Oct. 2000, nationalhumanitiescenter.org/tserve/twenty/tkeyinfo/trelww2.htm.

[19] Masci, David. "Why Millennials Are Less Religious than Older Americans." *Pew Research Center*, Pew Research Center, 30 May 2020, www.pewresearch.org/fact-tank/2016/01/08/qa-why-millennials-are-less-religious-than-older-americans/.

[20] In U.S., Decline of Christianity Continues at Rapid Pace." *Pew Research Center's Religion & Public Life Project*, 9 June 2020, www.pewforum.org/2019/10/17/in-u-s-decline-of-christianity-continues-at-rapid-pace/.

Unfortunately, many Christians seem to be intent on repeating the mistakes of the past.

As the new generation of socially minded Christians has taken up the mantle of reform, the Church's reaction has been mixed. While many find themselves on the frontlines of the past decades calls for justice, starting during the Occupy Wall Street movement and the ongoing Black Lives Matter movement, many of Christendom's most recognizable faces have been more reticent if not resistant.

Many pastors, black and white, have been vocal advocates for change while others have been slow to the punch perhaps for fear of backlash like the clergy of old. Popular evangelicals like Rod Parsley and Jerry Falwell have gone to bat for the country's institutions even, in the case of Parsley, seemingly defending the framers of the Constitution for owning slaves.[21]

Indeed, many evangelicals struggle with the idea that the Church ought to be the catalyst of social reform. Just about 1 in every 4 evangelicals does not support the Black Lives Matter movement[22] and those believers who do, aren't nearly as

---

[21] Blair, Leonardo. "Televangelist Rod Parsley under Fire for Claiming America's Founders Released All Their Slaves." *The Christian Post*, The Christian Post, 1 July 2020, www.christianpost.com/amp/televangelist-rod-parsley-under-fire-for-c laiming-americas-founders-released-all-their-slaves.html.

[22] Lee, Morgan. "Where John Piper and Other Evangelicals Stand on Black Lives Matter." *News & Reporting*, Christianity Today, 13 May 2016, www.christianitytoday.com/news/2016/may/where-john-piper-evange licals-stand-black-lives-matter-blm.html.

vociferous as their dissidents in the pews or even non-believing BLM supporters.

Less than 5% of Christians express support for the movement on social media in a given week.[23] Interestingly, according to that same study, majority of Christians across the board believe reverse racism is a problem (69%) and that the law is impartially applied to all races (63%).[24]

This is not so surprising considering the number of Christians who dismiss the BLM movement and its supporters with pejoratives like "antichrist" and "Marxist" despite many showing they lack knowledge of what Marxism is. What is just as conspicuous is the percentage of practicing Christians who believe the Church contributes to racial division (26%) compared to the 4 in 10 non-believers, including 43% of black respondents, who believe the same.[25]

Regardless of what role people may believe the Church is playing in the race issue, the survey indicates the vast majority of

---

[23] Lee, Morgan. "Where John Piper and Other Evangelicals Stand on Black Lives Matter." *News & Reporting*, Christianity Today, 13 May 2016, www.christianitytoday.com/news/2016/may/where-john-piper-evangelicals-stand-black-lives-matter-blm.html.

[24] Lee, Morgan. "Where John Piper and Other Evangelicals Stand on Black Lives Matter." *News & Reporting*, Christianity Today, 13 May 2016, www.christianitytoday.com/news/2016/may/where-john-piper-evangelicals-stand-black-lives-matter-blm.html.

[25] Lee, Morgan. "Where John Piper and Other Evangelicals Stand on Black Lives Matter." *News & Reporting*, Christianity Today, 13 May 2016, www.christianitytoday.com/news/2016/may/where-john-piper-evangelicals-stand-black-lives-matter-blm.html.

American adults (73%) believe the church should be active in fostering racial reconciliation.[26] Exactly how that reconciliation is engendered is a hard question to answer, but we will try to do so in a later chapter. Nevertheless, in the minds of most Americans, the Church hasn't lost its own opportunity for reconciliation with society.

The Church cannot and should not wait for the next killing of an unarmed black man, or the next protest against unfair labor practices, or the next rally for truly affordable healthcare to take a stand against institutional wickedness. I want to conclude by saying I believe people care for those who care for them. Perhaps this is not reality, but the perception that many people outside of Christendom have of the Church is that it cares very little for people and even less for those who aren't members.

For the Church to regain relevance, it must display a genuine concern for the people of which it is composed. It must prove itself an advocate for just causes and not a bystander or worse an obstacle. Perhaps doing so will encourage those who have dismissed the church as, in the words of Dr. King Jr., "an irrelevant social club with no meaning" to change their opinions. For all we know, they could be the next generation of pastors and church leaders, but we won't know that unless the Church does its part to win their hearts.

---

[26] Lee, Morgan. "Where John Piper and Other Evangelicals Stand on Black Lives Matter." *News & Reporting*, Christianity Today, 13 May 2016, www.christianitytoday.com/news/2016/may/where-john-piper-evange licals-stand-black-lives-matter-blm.html.

On the State of Humankind and the Origins of Government

Before we discuss the role of the modern Church, first we must discuss the role and origin of government, because I think the two are more similar than we may realize at first glance. Before we discuss government, however, we must discuss the state, nature, and origin of man:

> "To understand political power aright and derive it from its original, we must consider what estate all men are naturally in. A state of perfect freedom to order their actions and dispose of their possessions and persons as they think fit, within the bounds of the law of nature, without asking leave or depending upon the will of any other man".

All of humankind is, not-only born free, but with agency, the ability to create and execute one's own will. When God created man, he made us unique in that we are both a part of and apart from the rest of creation:

> Then God said, "Let Us (Father, Son, Holy Spirit) make man in Our image, according to Our likeness [not physical, but a spiritual personality and moral likeness]; and let them have complete authority over the fish of the sea, the birds of the air, the cattle, and over the entire earth, and over everything that creeps and crawls on the earth.

So God created man in His own image, the image, and likeness of God He created him; male and female He created them. And God blessed them [granting them certain authority] and said to them, "Be fruitful, multiply, and fill the earth, and subjugate it [putting it under your power]; and rule over (dominate) the fish of the sea, the birds of the air, and every living thing that moves upon the earth." (Gen 1:26-28 AMP)

So we were given both the agency and mandate of God to rule creation as we saw fit because we were essentially gods ourselves. We were naturally good, as God is, and because we were naturally good, we were naturally selfless, as God is. Therefore, our nature was to do what was in the best interests of ourselves, each other, and all of creation.

In other words, there was no need for a government because man was naturally good enough to govern himself without any central authority to look to for guidance. However, when sin entered the world, it corrupted man's nature. Man's nature was no longer all good. Man was no longer wholly altruistic. Instead, we became preoccupied with our own self-preservation:

"But the Lord God called to Adam, and said to him, Where are you? He said, "I heard the sound of You [walking] in the garden, and I was afraid because I was naked; so I hid myself. God said, 'Who told you that you were naked? Have you eaten [fruit] from the tree of which I commanded you not to eat? **And the man said,** The woman whom You gave to be with me—she gave me [fruit] from the tree, and I ate it. Then the Lord God said to the woman, What is this that you have done?'

And the woman said, The serpent beguiled and deceived me, and I ate [from the forbidden tree]. (Gen 3:9-13)

Notice how both Adam and Eve deflect blame for their offense to preserve themselves from God's wrath? From this point moving forward, the natural inclination of humankind was first and foremost self-preservation. This excerpt is one of the most well-known passages from Thomas Hobbes' *Leviathan*:

> "The right of nature, which writers commonly call jus naturale, is the liberty each man hath to use his own power as he will himself for the preservation of his own nature; that is to say, of his own life; and consequently, of doing anything which, in his own judgment and reason, he shall conceive to be the aptest means thereunto."[27]

This is the gift and the curse of agency, the freedom to make one's own decisions even if they are the wrong decisions. In this case, the decision of two doomed us to be bound by a new natural law, where self-preservation is prioritized above all else:

> "although they knew God, they did not glorify Him as God, nor were thankful, but became futile in their thoughts, and their foolish hearts were darkened. Professing to be wise, they became fools, and changed the glory of the incorruptible God into an image made like corruptible man...who exchanged the truth of God for the lie, and worshiped and served the creature rather than the Creator, who is blessed forever. Amen"

---

[27] Edward White and David Widger , "Leviathan, by Thomas Hobbes," The Project Gutenberg Ebook of Leviathan by Thomas Hobbes, October 11, 2009, https://gutenberg.org/files/3207/3207-h/3207h.htms)

(Rom 1:21-23, 25 NKJV)

Therefore, in the absence of government and according to natural law, I believe it is lawful to do whatever is necessary for self-preservation. Do I think it is constructive? No.

Do I think it is morally just? Again, no. In the words of the Apostle Paul, "All things are lawful unto me, but all things are not expedient: all things are lawful for me, but I will not be brought under the power of any." (1 Cor 6:12 KJV). Do I believe that man has no capacity for good in the absence of government? No.

I believe that man has the capacity for both goodness and evil as we are still created in the image and likeness of God; therefore, we have godlike qualities. When sin entered the world and disrupted God's natural order, it created in man the capacity for evil. I believe in the absence of a higher authority; a person will do good when convenient to them. I also believe a person can do evil when they deem it necessary to achieve their end.

> "For I know that in me (that is, in my flesh) nothing good dwells; for to will is present with me, but how to perform what is good I do not find. For the good that I will to do, I do not do; but the evil I will not to do, that I practice. Now if I do what I will not to do, it is no longer I who do it, but sin that dwells in me. I find then a law, that evil is present with me, the one who wills to do good." (Rom 7:18-21)

Part of the beauty and mystery of salvation is that this natural law does not bind us who are born in Christ. One might even argue it is the natural inclination of a true Christian to act not in his interests, but that of his fellow man, because it's what Christ would do:

"For the law of the Spirit of life in Christ Jesus has made me free from the law of sin and death. For what the law could not do in that it was weak through the flesh, God did by sending His own Son in the likeness of sinful flesh, on account of sin: He condemned sin in the flesh... For those who live according to the flesh set their minds on the things of the flesh, but those who live according to the Spirit, the things of the Spirit." (Rom 8:2-5 NKJV).

However, the word indicates the natural law still applies to those of us who continue to walk after the flesh and not the Spirit of God. To be like Christ is to be like God, and to be like God is to strive for goodness. However, though we may be in Christ, the world is not and, therefore, subject to the natural corrupted law of the flesh.

Because man's natural law prioritizes self-preservation, Thomas Hobbes describes the natural state of humankind as a continuous war of "everyone against everyone."[28] A state of continuous war between individuals is never a constructive one. Sure, it would be great to do what we please when we please as is our natural right, but is it really for the best? Can civilized society exists where continuous interpersonal strife exist?

"that a man be willing,...to lay down this right to all things, and be contented with so much liberty against other men as he would allow ...For as long as every man holdeth this right, of doing anything he liketh; so long are all men in the condition of war."[29]

---

[28] Edward White and David Widger , "Leviathan, by Thomas Hobbes," The Project Gutenberg Ebook of Leviathan by Thomas Hobbes, October 11, 2009,
https://gutenberg.org/files/3207/3207-h/3207h.htm)

[29] Edward White and David Widger , "Leviathan, by Thomas Hobbes," The Project Gutenberg Ebook of Leviathan by Thomas Hobbes, October 11, 2009,
https://gutenberg.org/files/3207/3207-h/3207h.htm)

It isn't constructive for the individuals, and it certainly isn't constructive for society. When everyone is busy fighting among themselves over whatever resources and perhaps, more importantly, the amount thereof they deem "necessary" for preservation, how does one have time to use them? When what one person believes is necessary for their own self-preservation requires intrusion upon another's efforts at the same, who or what determines who is right and who is wrong? This, according to John Locke, is the purpose of society:

> The great end of [men] entering into society [is] the enjoyment of their properties in peace and safety, and the great instrument and means of that being the laws established in that society, the first and fundamental positive law of all commonwealths is the establishing of the legislative power, as **the first and fundamental natural law [therefore purpose of government] ... is the preservation of the society.** [19]

And so here we have the purpose for government, mankind's protection against itself. We willfully enter into a contract in which we agree to sacrifice our right of and to everything, that we might be secured from each other's harm to our person and property. So let's say for the sake of argument we adhere to Locke's model, in the same way, the U.S. Constitution does, in that we establish and empower a central authority, and submit a portion of our natural rights to it. What happens when that authority misuses the power at the expense of the governed? There is an answer right in our Constitution:

> Governments are instituted among Men, deriving their just powers from the consent of the governed, --That whenever any Form of Government becomes

destructive of these ends, it is the Right of the People to alter or to abolish it

Let's take a moment and discuss the source from which authority derives its power. Notice the Constitution's use of the term "consent of the governed." That was not by accident. Whereas Hobbes advocated for absolute monarchy, and Locke for a constitutional monarchy, Jean Jacques Rousseau presented this model:

> "If then we discard from the social compact what is not of its essence, we shall find that it reduces itself to the following terms— Each of us puts his person and all his power in common under the supreme direction of the general will, and, in our corporate capacity, we receive each member as an indivisible part of the whole.[30]

Rousseau proposes a literal government of, by, and for the people. The sovereign (the ruler) of the people is the people themselves. So, according to this model, from where does the sovereign's sovereignty come? Consider the following:

> But the body politic or the sovereign drawing it is wholly from the sanctity of the contract can never bind itself. To an outsider, to do anything derogatory to the original act, for instance, to alienate any part of itself or submit to another sovereign. Violation of the act by which it exists would be self-annihilation, and that which is itself nothing can create nothing.

---

[30] Jean Jacques Rousseau , "The Social Contract - Early Modern Texts," accessed April 14, 2020, http://www.earlymoderntexts.com/assets/pdfs/rousseau1762.pdf) [22]

Though they disagreed on the literal structure of their proposed governments, Lock and Rousseau agreed that a government's authority came from the people's consent. So long as the government acted in the interests of its people, it maintained legitimacy.

Let me say now before we move any further; this is all theoretical. Governments existed before Hobbes, Locke, and Rousseau, and the concepts of both democracy and republicanism are as ancient as classical Greece and Rome. Though I may disagree, I have known people who have argued quite persuasively that people can govern themselves. However, the impact these theories have had on government and its application are undeniable. Consider this article from the Universal Declaration of Human Rights drafted by the United Nations in 1948:

> The will of the people shall be the basis of the authority of government; this will shall be expressed in periodic and genuine elections which shall be by universal and equal suffrage and shall be held by secret vote or by equivalent free voting procedures.[31]

So based upon this declaration, I believe two things:

1. A government's authority is only legitimate if the people it governs deem it so, by consenting to be governed by it.

---

[31] "Universal Declaration of Human Rights," United Nations (United Nations), accessed April 14, 2020, http://www.un.org/en/universaldeclaration-human-rights/index.html)

2. The governed should only consent to a government's authority if that government acts in the interests of all the people

I want to emphasize "all" because history has proven that government, when gone unchecked, can act in the interests of a few particularly influential, often wealthy people. I believe a government should never be composed entirely of or directly connected to any group of people, especially when that group prioritizes its interests above the interests, and at the expense of others. The government ought to treat all governed parties as equals, even those of which it is composed.

The government's purpose should be to protect and preserve everyone's rights and protection from exploitation. The government's purpose ought not to be authority for authority's sake. It most certainly ought not to be for its own self-preservation or interests. Unfortunately, this is what happens when we allow the government to go unchecked by the public. It will, like all other natural bodies, begin to prioritize its interest or, more specifically, the parties of which it is composed or influenced, above all else.

I know that I am being repetitive, but I'm doing so to drive home a point. The government's inherent purpose is to preserve and protect the people, but the people's inherent purpose is not to preserve the government. Furthermore, no government has an inherent right to rule or even exists. Its right comes directly from its willingness and capacity to serve and protect the people. The people should only seek to preserve a government if doing so is indisputably in their best interests.

Now ask yourself this. What is a church, if not a form of government? I'm speaking specifically about the host of organized assemblies we call the Church. Local, regional, nationally organized institutions, the host of different denominations and organizations within those denominations, are these not governmental bodies? With that established, what does a government do?

It creates laws and enforces laws (which maintain order) and creates policy (which provide guidance for the creation of laws) So why does a church (i.e., governing body) exists if not to fulfill these ends? Does the Church not fulfill the same function for the body of Christ that secular governments do for society? Therefore, should not the same principles of legitimacy that apply to the secular government not apply to a church?

I believe members should do all that is in their power to preserve the organized body if it is in their holistic interests, but primarily the spiritual. However, far too often, we burden membership with the preservation of the organized body for no other reason than for preservation's sake. For this reason, many members of organized bodies question the purpose of not only the Church, but themselves within the Church. Many members are left unfulfilled because they are constantly asked, whether implicitly or explicitly, to sacrifice their agency for the sake of the Church's.

This is also the reason why many non-believers dismiss the purpose of an organized religious body and therefore are not receptive to any solicitation from organized religion.[32]

---

[32] Holly Meyer, "What New LifeWay Research Survey Says about Why

.

Now I know that opponents of this stance will argue that the Church's authority comes not from its members but from God, to which I agree. However, for what purpose is that authority given if not for the people's spiritual interests? Therefore, if a body does not act in the express interests of the people, where does it draw its legitimacy?

> Now it is up to you. Be on your toes—both for yourselves and your congregation of sheep. The Holy Spirit has put you in charge of these people—God's people they are— to guard and protect them. God himself thought they were worth dying for (Acts 20:28 AMP)

> "For God is not unjust so as to forget your work and the love which you have shown for His name in ministering to [the needs of] the saints (God's people), as you do." (Heb 6:10 AMP)

With all that being said, I would like to conclude this chapter by making the following statement: A church's (i.e., organized body of believers) inherent purpose is to serve God by serving his people. However, people's inherent purpose is not to serve the Church. Therefore, no organized body has an inherent right to govern God's people or even to exist except if it is in the explicit

---

Young Adults Are Dropping out of Church," The Tennessean (The Tennessean, January 15, 2019), https://www.tennessean.com/story/news/religion/2019/01/15/lifewa y-research-survey-says-young-adults-dropping-outchurch/2550997002 /)

interest of the saints. Its authority comes from God by way of its ability and willingness to serve God's people.

In order to revive its relevance, the modern Church must embrace this philosophy and seek to fulfill the holistic interests of all God's children even at its own expense. If it does, society will understand that losing the Church's presence would be disastrous to its spiritual and natural wellbeing.

On the Use of Narrative Control

As I've argued in the previous chapter, the government's purpose is to serve the people. A government ought not to become unchecked to the point it develops its own agency and loses its purpose. That government will create its own interests and seek to preserve those interests as opposed to the interests of the people it governs, and even at the expense of the people it governs. That government will then have the potential to misuse the authority vested in it and use the people it governs as means to its own end.

A government of, by, or, for the people, however, cannot abuse the people without the people's consent. Once again, the people's will is what keeps that government intact. So before such a government can enforce its own will upon the governed, it must first suppress the governed's ability and or desire to express dissent.[33]

I want to spend the next chapters discussing how entities suppress dissent. I want to talk to you about control, in this case narrative control, how it's used and how it's accomplished. How often have you heard the phrase "history is written by the victors"? How often have you questioned the validity of what you've read, what you've heard, or what you've been taught?

Have you ever asked a question, say for example "where do babies come from?" and you asked what you assumed was a reliable source and they weaved together a story that to you sounded like it made sense, and so you did not question that narrative only to find out much later down the line that their

---

[33] Herbert Marcuse, *One-Dimensional Man* (London: Routledge, 2002))

narrative was false? Now what if despite your discovery to the contrary, this formerly reliable source insists that babies in fact come from storks?

Let's say for the sake of argument this reliable source is very much aware of how erroneous the narrative is, but it perpetuates the narrative not because it benefits directly from the narrative itself, but the belief in it as trustworthy? What do you believe is the most logical outcome in this scenario? Some of you will argue that in the name of the moral good, that source will bite the bullet, accept its error, and change its narrative.

This is assuming such an entity would prioritize the moral good, but what history has proven to us is that government rarely prioritizes moral over practical good unless pressed to do so by those whom it governs. I believe this scenario is even less likely in the event the entity risks losing its mandate to govern which again is the purpose for its existence. This is why narrative control is so important.

There is a possibility that a government that has developed its own interests would do whatever is in its power to promote those interests would conflict with the governed's best interests. Furthermore, is it not right to assume that that same government would do what is in its power to promote and protect a narrative that paints it and the system it depends upon as a) morally just b) in the interest of the people c) trustworthy?

In the context of legitimacy, the actual truth matters very little. It matters less that one is truthful and more that one is perceived as such.

As long as one is deemed trustworthy, there is little reason to question the validity of whatever narrative is being told. In the context of the U.S. government, It has not been until recently that many of people have been given a reason to question the narrative of the central authority only because it is so blatantly and audaciously dishonest. Even with the previous administration's total disregard for the truth, there remains a contingent of people who accept that administration's version of the truth as truth.

Now the point can be argued that this contingent is less concerned with actual truth than they are with their truth being the preferred narrative. The point can also be argued that many feel powerless to do anything regarding the narrative. Therefore, against their conscience, they accept the narrative as truth. The fact remains, in regard to legitimacy, as long as the majority of the governed accepts the narrative as truth, the actual truth matters very little. In other words, in regard to the right to rule, the majority's opinion is truth.

And as long as an entity can control the narrative in a way that paints itself in a positive light, it is empowered to act as it pleases even if its actions are in direct conflict with the governed's interests. As long as we believe the government is acting in the interest of the people, the government maintains its mandate. This is why the easiest way to control any population is by controlling the narrative. Once again, I'm being repetitive but that is the teacher in me.

Authoritarian regimes primarily use two tactics to control a narrative, propaganda, and fear. According to Encyclopedia Brittanica, "propaganda is dissemination of information—facts, arguments, rumours, half-truths, or lies—to influence public opinion."[34] Propaganda is not inherently nefarious, but it is manipulative. We are exposed to propaganda every day most times, not even realizing it. Advertisers, politicians, even our friends, and families use propaganda to control a narrative and garner their desired response. Would you believe if I suggested the modern Church is not immune?

Perhaps you've noticed the King James translation of the Bible has fallen out of favor with many Christians. I'll admit I'm one of those Christians, because parts of that translation, and all translations honestly, can be called propaganda. By the time King James VI had come to the throne of England in the early 17th century, there were several translations percolating through Christendom. The most popular of these was the Geneva Bible called "History's First Study Bible"[35]

This translation was popular for two reasons. It was the first generally available mass-produced Bible featuring many of the quality of life features we take for granted. These features included the first instances of verses and chapters to make reading easier, but also chapter summarizations, scriptural cross-references, study guides, illustrations, tables, commentaries, maps, and others.[36] The second reason is that

---

[34] Bruce Lannes Smith, "Propaganda," Encyclopædia Britannica (Encyclopædia Britannica, inc., March 20, 2020), https://www.britannica.com/topic/propaganda)

[35] Daniel Reichard , "The 1599 Geneva Bible: History's First Study Bible," Bible Gateway Blog (Bible Gateway , June 7, 2018), https://www.biblegateway.com/blog/2017/10/the-1599-genevabible-historys-first-study-bible/)

[36] Daniel Reichard , "The 1599 Geneva Bible: History's First Study Bible," Bible Gateway Blog (Bible Gateway , June 7, 2018),

the notes and aides I mentioned were written by reformers. In fact, the Geneva Bible was based in large part on a translation written by Protestant reformers who were, to put it generously, critical of the Church hierarchy:

> "...its circulation threatened the Anglican bishops. Not only did the Geneva Bible supplant their translation...but it also appeared to challenge the primacy of secular rulers and the bishops' authority. One of its scathing annotations compared the locusts of the Apocalypse to swarming hordes of "Prelates" dominating the Church.[37]

Other annotations referred to the Apostles and Christ himself as "holy fools," an approving phrase meant to evoke their disdain for "all outward pompe" in contrast to the supposed decadence of the Anglican and Catholic Churches."[38] To bring the Bishops of the Church of England and the Protestant reformers together in compromise (and to establish the legitimacy of the social and clerical hierarchy and primacy of the King), King James commissioned a new translation that would borrow from both the Geneva and Bishops' translations. This "King James Translation" was made available to the public in 1611. [39]

---

https://www.biblegateway.com/blog/2017/10/the-1599-genevabible-historys-first-study-bible

[37] Joel L Levy, *Time* (Time USA LLC, June 19, 2017), https://time.com/4821911/king-james-bible-history/)

[38] Joel L Levy, *Time* (Time USA LLC, June 19, 2017), https://time.com/4821911/king-james-bible-history/)

[39] Joel L Levy, *Time* (Time USA LLC, June 19, 2017), https://time.com/4821911/king-james-bible-history/)

I still enjoy the KJV translation. It's still my preferred translation when I prepare a message, but for study, I try not to rely on it because I know certain passages were written for a purpose to which I am opposed. Propaganda is powerful because most of us frankly take whatever we hear, see, and read at face value. Be honest, how many of you reading this book will really look at any of, let alone all, the sources and references I've used for research?

That's why I made it a point to transcribe most of the scriptural reference I've used for this book, so no one reading it would just draw their conclusion on my arguments alone or assume my exegesis is based on conjecture. That's what critical thinking is all about, looking at the sources and forming an organic opinion on a subject. That's what this book is all about, encouraging you to form an organic opinion.

Unfortunately, some governments (including churches) would rather keep their governed subject to collective consciousness than facilitate independent thought. Any entity that discourages independent thought is a danger to those it governs. Propaganda could come in the form of association. One is conditioned to associate a particular word, phrase, or image with a positive or negative feeling (i.e. MAGA, the Obama "HOPE" poster).

It can come in the form of omitting certain facts from your message to paint yourself or product in the best light, telling "half-truths". It can come in what advertisers call "band wagoning", in other words peer pressure. It can come in the form of hatemongering by appealing to one's prejudices, which we all have. It can be plastered on posters, broadcasts over radio waves and television. It can even be shared over the web and through social media. Traditionally when we think of propaganda, we think of state-run media outlets, war bond posters, and the like, but I think the most dangerous propaganda is the sort we make ourselves.

Recall not so long-ago people all across the country and world expressed outrage over a pattern of police brutality toward black males and, more importantly, the lack of response to these actions. Do you recall what happened when people began to express dissent? It was not the government that suppressed the Black Lives Matter movement, but it was our fellow Americans. Black Lives Matter became an anti-police movement. For some, it even became an anti-white movement, and so began slogans like "Blue Lives Matter" and "All Lives Matter".

Rarely do you hear of so-called black on black crime unless it's used as deflection against those decrying systemic racism. Athletes became unpatriotic and even treasonous for protesting what they considered to be a gross injustice. I won't argue the reasoning behind such reactions, but I will say this is one of the best and most recent examples of suppression through propaganda, perpetuated by the people no less.

History teaches us that the Church is not immune to these practices. I gave you one of the most enduring examples earlier. How many assemblies have drafted their laws according to the KJV translation with every intent to govern in a biblically sound manner, unwittingly fulfilling the very purpose the translators intended which again, was to maintain the clerical and secular hierarchy of that day. Particularly in more traditionalist congregations, we discourage dissent among members, both clergy and laity. We do so when we wax nostalgic about the Church of our parents' and grandparents' day and their virtues while omitting their failures from our narrative.

We do it when we see a brother or sister has been absent, and we call them "fair weather" or "unfaithful" without even knowing the cause of their absence. We do it when we use generalities like "for the up building of the ministry" or "kingdom building" to justify the giving of our time, energy, and money to the Church without specifying exactly how our gifts and sacrifices will do that. We do it when we shun brother and sisters who have changed their membership to another assembly.

We do so when we deify our leaders by deeming their word as unquestionable and infallible. I grew up in a traditionalist ministry and even today am part of a traditionalist organization. I have heard my entire life the phrase "blessings come down" or "from the head" or even "to the pastor first" as if to imply some system of spiritual Reganomics is at work. That phrase to this day doesn't sit very well with me because it implies one is out of step with God if one is not in unquestioned submission to church leadership by virtue of nothing more than the leader's status as leader.

How can this be when Jesus said there is no master, no teacher, no Lord but himself? How can this be when God said his glory, he would not share with anyone? How can this be when Jesus taught us that we are all equal brothers and sisters in Christ? Yes, God has set leaders over us to guide us in the right path, but does that make a leader a ruler? And if not, why imply as much?

All of this helps to perpetuate the narrative that the Church, particularly its leadership, is infallible and unquestionable.

Many Christians use this narrative as the reason why we don't share Jesus. It's never because there's anything wrong with, or in the Church, but that there's something wrong with everyone else and it's that they simply don't want Jesus. "They don't want to be saved, they want to live in sin, they don't want to live holy, they don't want to hear the truth unless it's their truth." These are the excuses we make regularly. Ironic considering how many of us refuse to believe that maybe we're the ones resistant to truth.

I want to end this chapter by talking about fear. Whereas propaganda is indirect and subtle, fear is blatant and direct but somehow just as, if not more effective than more subtle means of control. It is common knowledge that authoritarian regimes reward dissent with severe repercussion. Sometimes it is as simple as a minor inconvenience here or there, others it is something more serious, something that could threaten one's livelihood or even life. In this state, propaganda might not be necessary because the fear of retaliation will stop any dissent before it comes about. It may even cause one to become hostile toward those bold enough to dissent for fear that their actions will bring harm upon the whole community.

Too often, we in the Church allow fear to keep us quiet. We allow fear to keep us from expressing our concern when we see something wrong in ministry. Some of us are afraid of ruining the friendships we've come to cherish. Some of us are afraid of losing out on promotion by rubbing the wrong people the wrong way. Some of us are afraid of what people would say behind closed doors or think in the privacy of their minds about us, what rumors they will spread what gossip they will share what secrets they will reveal. Some of us are so conditioned that we hold our tongue fearing the wrath of God himself would come on us if we ever thought of the Church in anything less than a glowing manner:

> "Brothers, if anyone is caught in any sin, you who are spiritual [that is, you who are responsive to the guidance of the Spirit] are to restore such a person in a spirit of gentleness [not with a sense of superiority or self-righteousness], keeping a watchful eye on yourself, so that you are not tempted as well. Carry one another's burdens and in this way you will fulfill the requirements of the law of Christ [that is, the law of Christian love]." (Gal 6:2 AMP)

The first step to fixing any problem is accepting that the problem exists. Sometimes we need a little help doing that. Remember, our goal as Christians should never be to catch someone in sin so we can lord it over them. Our desire should never be to condemn but to improve. I have a rule, and that rule is I never draw attention to a problem unless I have a suggestion for a solution and am willing to work toward the solution. This way I don't fall into the trap of self-righteousness. We ought to sincerely desire the best for one another and help each other become the absolute best we can be. We cannot do that if we're always turning a blind eye to faults. That is not love. That is enablement. If we are to be Christ-like and Christ, because he loves us, corrects us when we are at fault, then we should not be afraid or made to be afraid to do the same.

On the Dangers of a Distraction and Disinterest

Assuming you believe, as I do, a government's authority comes from the consent of the people to be governed. You should also believe that a government can only be as powerful as the governed will allow it to be. Therefore, if a government ever becomes so powerful as to be unquestionable, it is because the governed have allowed it to become so. If a government's purpose is corrupted to serve either the interests of itself or a few, it is not the government's fault but the governed.

> "It[legislative authority] is not, nor can be arbitrary over the lives and fortunes of the people, for it being but the joint power of every member of the society given up to that... [governing authority]; it can be no more than those persons had in a state of nature before they entered into society and gave up to the community: for nobody can transfer to another more power than he has in himself; and no [legislative] body has an absolute arbitrary [by random] power over [it]self, or over any other, to destroy his own life, or take away the life or property of another... [40]

So the question is, why would society ever allow its government to become so powerful and or corrupted it loses its purpose. The answer is because the people were too distracted or too disinterested to prevent it from doing so. Because it is human nature to seek the path of least resistance, Americans have a history and now a condition to sacrifice freedoms for the sake of

---

[40] John Locke, "Second Treatise of Government - Early Modern Texts," accessed April 14, 2020,
http://www.earlymoderntexts.com/assets/pdfs/locke1689a.pdf)

convenience. Therefore I believe, despite the unprecedented interconnectivity the internet has given us, direct democracy would never work in this country.

I bring that up because theoretically, we could cast our ballots from our devices whenever a referendum took place. However, if we are going to be honest with ourselves, many of us are too ill-informed on most issues to create policy. This is despite unlimited access to information that is right at our fingertips. Instead, we entrust this freedom to our representatives; this should work, but once again, our lack of engagement causes this system to fail, and as a millennial, I would like to point out that it is not just young people. Across the board, American election turnouts are among the worse in the developed world.

> The 55.7% VAP turnout in 2016 puts the U.S. behind most of its peers in the Organization for Economic Cooperation and Development (OECD), most of whose members are highly developed, democratic states. Looking at the most recent nationwide election in each OECD nation, the U.S. placed 26th out of 32 Drew Desilver, "U.S. Trails Most Developed Countries In Voter Turnout, ,"[41]

Considering that 2016 was a national election that always draws a greater turnout than state or local elections, the numbers are even more damning. Granted, the 2016 election garnered the worse voter turnout in U.S. history (due in large part to dissatisfaction with both candidates); however, prior to the most recent Presidential election, turnout has never gone above 60% of eligible voters since 1968.[33] Now I'm sure by now you have

---

[41] Drew Desilver, "US Trails Most Developed Countries In Voter Turnout, ," Factank (Pew Research Center, May 21, 2018), https://www.pewresearch.org/fact-tank/2018/05/21/u-s-voterturnout-trails-most-developed-countries/)

heard or read of how to 2020 Presidential election saw record turnout. This is true but again, the percentage of eligible voters who actually did vote was in the low 60th percentile (it must also be voted that this election was unique for a myriad of reasons we don't have time to get into). Now there are several reasons why people do not or cannot vote that are completely understandable. However, the fact remains

We used the phrase "religion is the people's opium" a few times now. To an extent, I agree. Of course, opioids are depressants, pain killers, sedatives, downers. They numb one to the pain brought upon them by their condition, but they never address the illness itself, only the symptoms. Religion serves as a painkiller for the believer and too often in the contemporary Church, nothing more than that.

As an institution, we've become addicted to religion at the expense of spirituality and our sensitivity to the groans of the world and the people who live in it. However, this religion we practice is not one in which the God of the scriptures is the god we worship. No wealth is, and the possession of it, the pursuit of it, the use of it—wealth in the literal and metaphorical sense. Holistic self-wellness is the popular theology of the day, and this is a direct result of the Church adopting the capitalistic self-interested philosophy of mainstream society. However, this chapter is not about that.

We are talking about the secular world's opiate, which is consumption, and yes there is a difference. This country and the people in it became so wealthy so fast that we barely knew what to do with the spoils of the post-WWII economic boom. Since then, our lives have become fixated upon entertainment and leisure. Seemingly overnight new industries began to sprout up explicitly for the consumption of the two. America became and is still a country obsessed with consumption to the point it dominates our collective consciousness. Some might even argue, creating a "false consciousness":

> The means of communication, the irresistible output of the entertainment and information industry carry with them prescribed attitudes and habits, certain intellectual and emotional reactions which bind the consumers to the producers and, through the latter to the whole social system. The products indoctrinate and manipulate; they promote a false consciousness which is immune against its falsehood...[42]

When I first read this book (One Dimensional Man written by Herbert Marcuse), I was convinced that I had finally found the answer to why things are the way they are. I was convinced that a conscious and cooperative plan was being executed by the government and special interests, corporate interests, in particular, and had suppressed the people's ability to dissent by jacking us all into the Matrix. So convicted was I that one of my first messages, after I returned to the Lord and began preaching, was titled "The One-Dimensional Church". However, today, I am not so sure.

I agree with Marcuse that consumption distracts us from things that matter. I agree that the constant flow of consumer goods creates a false need for the latest and greatest of those goods, and yes, I agree that these goods have become directly tied to our sense of self (which I will elaborate on in a later chapter). I am no longer convinced; this false consciousness is a coordinated attempt by the government or even special interest

---

[42] Herbert Marcuse, *One-Dimensional Man pp-12* (London: Routledge, 2002)

groups. I am not even convinced this false consciousness is even false.

I am convinced to be completely ill or misinformed in the information age, is to be so willingly. We are constantly bombarded with information through traditional, and perhaps more so, through non-traditional media. The internet made it so that anyone with a voice can be heard, and anyone with ears to hear can listen. Even in our attempts to stem the flow of information into our minds, we cannot help but retain some of it. What we do retain is typically that which is necessary to satisfy our need to consume. With this great access to information, there has come a greater capacity for the consumption of material and immaterial goods.

Now because it would be impractical to retain all the information given to us, we have given a greater portion of that responsibility to the government. Therefore, we the people have entered into an unspoken agreement, a new social contract. In exchange for the responsibility of information, we have given the government the right to autonomy, so long as it does not impede our ability or right to consume.

Sometimes we choose to ignore the truth; we willfully jack into the Matrix to escape the ugliness around us. Humans have an incredible capacity to grow comfortable in discomfort. Unfortunately, the effect it has can be devastating when the government is allowed to run unchecked. I think the perfect example of this is the housing crisis of '08. This is not something that happened overnight, but years of many blind eyes being turned to the mortgage industry's unscrupulous actions.

Then when the chickens did come home to roost and the bubble burst, people had no choice but to pay attention and start asking some hard questions. When no sufficient answer was given, the people acted out in anger in the form of protests and demonstrations that became the Occupy Wall Street Movement. I know, I was there. This is what I believe; angry people are active people. If you want to get someone angry, mess with their wallet. Across the globe people are angry and are expressing that anger through protest, a form of dissent. I want you to consider this:

> In March 2019, Axios released results from a Harris poll showing that about half of millennial and Generation Z respondents believed that "our economy should be mostly socialist." That result is no outlier, but rather a consistent finding over recent years. In 2018, Gallup found that 51 percent of 18- to 29-year-old Americans view Socialism favorably; only 45 percent look at Capitalism positively. An August 2018 YouGov poll revealed that only 30 percent of 18- to 29-year-olds had good feelings toward Capitalism, while 35 percent regarded socialism positively[43]

Now consider this:

> Census family income data show that the era of shared prosperity ended in the 1970s... from 1979 to 2007 (just before the financial crisis and Great Recession), average income after transfers and taxes quadrupled for the top 1 percent of the distribution. The increases

[43] Edward L Glaeser, "How To Talk To Millenials About Capitalism ," City Journal (Manhattan Institute of Public Policy, April 2019), https://www.city-journal.org/millennials-embrace-socialism)

[36] Chad Stone et al., "A Guide to Statistics on Historical Trends in Income Inequality," Center on Budget and Policy Priorities (Center on Budget and Policy Priorities , February 11, 2020), https://www.cbpp.org/research/poverty-and-inequality/a-guide-tostatistics-on-historical-trends-in-income-inequality)

were much smaller for the middle 60 percent and bottom 20 percent of the distribution [...] the share of wealth held by the top 1 percent rose from just under 30 percent in 1989 to 38.6 percent in 2016, while the share held by the bottom 90 percent fell from 33.2 percent to 22.8 percent. Chad Stone et al., "A Guide to Statistics on Historical Trends in Income Inequality,"

Now, if we consider the accepted time frame for millennial birth dates (early 80s to mid 90s), it is not hard to figure out why we have seen an uptick in active dissent against advanced Capitalism in the last decade. I understand if this book reads as an indictment against the Church, and in part, it is. That is perhaps the reason you've made it this far. If this book is an indictment upon the Church, then it is also an indictment against the people who compose it. All that we have discussed thus far should lead us to this conclusion. The church (organized body) is only as powerful as the saints allow it to be. So, for all the faults and issues we find with our local, regional, national, and international bodies, the fault ultimately lies with us. The sooner we accept that, the sooner we can return to relevance.

I want you to look in the mirror and ask yourself if you have dedicated yourself as best you can to your purpose in ministry. How often have we distracted ourselves with Church business away from God's business? How often have we seen a problem in our churches, or our community go unaddressed and said, "let them handle it"? How many times have we been more concerned with membership than discipleship?

How many days have we spent absorbed in our devices, social accounts, and television sets, leaving us oblivious to the pitiful state of the world? How often have we sat in silence at the face of injustice because it had no direct effect on our churches or us? We have allowed our secular interests and sensibilities to distract us from and corrupt our personal and corporate ministries for too long.

We have turned our sanctuaries into fortresses, in which we shutter ourselves from the world, and our responsibility to its people through the high of the worship experience. Many ministers have been reduced to little more than holy hype men, inciting a praise break and preaching a sweet sedative by any means necessary even at the cost of a substantive word. This leaves many saints leaving the service happy but empty, ill-equipped to serve themselves or others. This does not account for the number of saints too distracted by their devices when the praise break has begun to even participate.

Now we look up, and we see our churches dwindling in membership because of our self-indulgence. Our ministries, both corporate and singular, have become self-indulgent. We took the concept of "preaching to the choir" to its zenith. When we step to the podium on a Sunday morning, many of us have no one to preach to except the choir. What is most disheartening is the fact that many of us are not as disturbed as we should be until our ineffectiveness begins to threaten as the bible says our "place and nation."

Because our churches are empty, because young people are leaving the church, and worse, finding no reason to return, many churches find themselves facing a very uncertain if not bleak future. The silent agreement we made to society to stay in our churches and away from directly confronting the wickedness of its institutions has come back to bite us:

"often, the contemporary church is a weak, ineffectual voice with an uncertain sound... Far from being disturbed by the church's presence, the power structure of the average community is consoled by the church's silent...sanction of things as they are [that is social injustice]. However, the judgment of God is upon the church as never before. Suppose today's church does not recapture the sacrificial spirit of the early church. In that case, it will lose its authenticity, forfeit the loyalty of millions, and be dismissed as an irrelevant social club with no meaning for the twentieth century." [44]

Ominous words from who is, in my opinion, the most consequential clergyman and theologian of the 20th century, but what disturbs me most is that this was written in 1963, which is nearly 60 years ago. It begs the question, at what point do we as the body of Christ realize how pitiful our state has become? We must corporately and individually make a commitment to serving all of God's children.

This begins with feeding the hungry, visiting the sick, shut-in, forgotten, and imprisoned, giving to the poor and sheltering the homeless and defending migrants, but it shouldn't stop there. We must commit ourselves as individuals and as a body to civic engagement. We must be active participants in the electoral and legislative process at every level. We must not settle for merely being the electors but the elected as well.

We must not be spectators and speculators but difference makers. We must make an individual and corporate commitment to combating injustice everywhere both de facto

---

[44] Martin L King, ed. Ali B Ali-Dinar, Letter from a Birmingham Jail [King, Jr.] (University of Pennsylvania), accessed April 14, 2020, https://www.africa.upenn.edu/Articles_Gen/Letter_Birmingham.html)

and de jure. We must combat the forces of evil not only on our knees but also in the voting booth, on the picket lines and borderlines, in the halls of the legislature and the halls of the prison, in the courtrooms and board rooms and wherever else injustice is.

We must not misuse worship in the same manner an addict uses an opioid, as a sedative numbing us to the world around us, but rather as a steroid empowering us to do the things our flesh is too weak to do on its own. We must not allow ourselves to become so preoccupied with the ceremony and mechanics of "having church", that we lose our purpose, which is to serve God by serving his creation:

> "I hate, I despise and reject your [sacred] feasts, And I do not take delight in your solemn assemblies. Even though you offer Me your burnt offerings and your grain offerings, I will not accept them; And I will not even look at the peace offerings of your fattened animals. Take the noise of your songs away from Me [they are an irritation]! I shall not even listen to the melody of your harps. But let justice run down like waters And righteousness like an ever-flowing stream [flowing abundantly]. (Amos 5:21-24 AMP)

We can no longer require membership as a prerequisite to service. We can no longer reduce ministry to only that which is comfortable, familiar, and convenient. We can no longer choose our battles according to our personal interests, but according to what is morally right and wrong. We must let our light shine so 2 all God's children can know his love through ours. There are those who do and will say so, and I commend you for your service, but this must be a concentrated cooperative effort by all of Christendom if we are to regain our relevance in this world.

On The Social Effects of Capitalism

Before we begin, let me stress this chapter is not meant to critique Capitalism's merits or flaws. I think it's been done much more effectively than I could do by much smarter people. Though this book has heavy political and sociological overtones, the primary purpose for an audience of this book is the Church; I am going to address Capitalism's impact on spiritual, moral, and sociological wellness.

In a perfect world, Capitalism would work for everyone, as would every other modern economic system. We do not live in a perfect world; otherwise, there would be no need for any system. The Achilles' heel of almost every world system is their failure to account for human nature adequately. In a perfect world, all things remain constant; there are no variables. Therefore, many systems, while good on paper, fail IRL. Real-world Capitalism has an advantage over any other system, for example, Communism in that it appeals to the variables rather than ignores or diminishes their role. It does this through the perceived "fairness" of its individualistic merit-based system of free enterprise.

Who could argue against a system that says you can and deserve to keep what you earn? How can you argue against a system that says, "What's yours ought to be yours and no one else's"? Although this is contrary to how Christ has taught us to live (Luke 14:13-14), I can see the merits in such a system. It is only fair after all. Now we can see that Capitalism's advantage is that it appeals to and utilizes the greed of men or self-interest, seemingly for the benefit of all, by presenting an even exchange of goods and services as its foundation. Consider this quote from Adam Smith, the father of modern Capitalism:

> "But man has almost constant occasion for the help of his brethren, and it is in vain for him to expect it from their benevolence only. He will be more likely to prevail if he can interest their self-love in his favour and show them that it is for their own advantage to do for him what he requires of them. Whoever offers to another a bargain of any kind, proposes to do this. Give me that which I want, and you shall have this which you want, is the meaning of every such offer; and it is in this manner that we obtain from one another the far greater part of those good offices which we stand in need of. It is not from the benevolence of the butcher, the brewer, or the baker that we expect our dinner, but from their regard to their own interest. We address ourselves, not to their humanity but to their self-love, and never talk to them of our own necessities but of their advantages. Nobody but a beggar chooses to depend chiefly upon the benevolence of his fellow-citizens. Even a beggar does not depend upon it entirely." [45]

The unfortunate truth is that Smith is right. It is entirely in our nature to do that, which is most beneficial in achieving our own end. Even if that end is to see others succeed, it is because it is something we desire to happen. Before we go any further, I want to make a few things clear.

I do not believe humans are inherently selfish or greedy, just self-interested. I will argue that society has facilitated an environment in which self-interestedness can easily be turned to selfishness and greed. The scarcity of resources and private ownership require our self-interests to be self-centered more often than not if we desire to maintain self-preservation. What

---

[45] Adam Smith, "Wealth of Nations in PDF for Free," ed. Mark Biernat, Political Economy (Political Economy, July 23, 2019), https://politicaleconomy.com/wealth-of-nations-adam-smith/)

makes the idea of Capitalism work is that most of us have learned to accept this truth, and therefore even if we wish things were different, the nature of man (self-interestedness) makes this system the most practical one.

However, notice I said the "idea" of Capitalism because that is what most capitalists hold unto as justification for the system. I believe Capitalism benefits from the illusion of fairness, the idea that it works and works for most people when done right. I believe most people will agree that there are flaws in the system. However, the failure is not in the system according to capitalists, but the few who exploit and the many who are not industrious or committed enough to make it work for themselves.

The stains on human history that have been facilitated by Capitalism that include the Trans-Atlantic slave trade, colonialism, the Gilded Age of the robber barons, and more recent stains such as: income inequality and disparities, the prison and military-industrial complexes, the housing crisis of the mid 00's, and the current health crisis in communities of color have been rationalized as the result of a handful of unscrupulous people exploiting the system. This is what capitalists will argue, it's not the game that's broken, but the players. I believe such a claim is only a half-truth, and secondly, I would argue such a claim can be made for every world system even the favorite target of many Capitalism defenders, Socialism.

Many point to Stalin or Mao as examples of Socialist systems' inherent danger despite both being Socialist in name only and in China's case, operating in what is in my and the opinion of others, a state-run Capitalist system. Perhaps Cuba is a better example of how and why Socialism does not work. Not discounting Castro's failures as both a humanitarian and statesman, consider the U.S.'s direct intervention in Cuba. Consider the plethora of failed assassination attempts that no doubt cause Castro to grow paranoid and suspicious of opposition and the 50-year embargo that helped decimate Cuba's economy.

You will see there is more to the picture than what meets the eye. I believe Capitalism's reputation continues to be a mostly positive one in this country because of its illusion of fairness; it never promises to work for everyone, only those willing to put the work in to make it work. Even though, often, this is not the case due to human nature, specifically the greater capacity for greed possessed by some.

Before we move any further, I want to make something clear. Though the term Marxism has been used by some believers as pejorative designed to engender fear of anti-Christian infiltration of the faith, Marxism is not that. Marxism is a school of thought that argues the working class' quality of life has been diminished through exploitation in the form of wage slavery and detachment from the means of production and the capital produced by it. Now to disagree with that school of thought is one thing, but the issue I find with most arguments by believers concerning Marxism is that they don't argue against the above philosophy because opponents are often ill or misinformed on what Marxism actually is.

I've seen arguments claiming Marxism to be everything from an occultist attack on the nuclear family to an anti-Christian new world order conspiracy. It's true his theory argued that material creates consciousness and thus the spiritual is a mere reflection of the natural mind (dialectical materialism). It is also true that he advocated for the eventual abolition of organized religion.[46] However, Marx like many other secular theorists did not completely dismiss the value of religion in society. Marx believed religion was a necessary, but temporary sedative for the misery experienced by the working class. This is evidenced in the often-misquoted phrase found in his 1844 work *A Contribution to Critique of Hegel's Philosophy of the Right*, "Religion is the sigh of the oppressed creature, the heart of a heartless world, and the soul of soulless conditions. It is the opium of the people."[47]

This chapter is not meant to be an apologetic for Marxism as it does have flaws and has yet to be applied successfully in the manner that Marx envisioned. It simply serves to level the playing field. Because, for as much criticism that is leveled by believers against Marxism, rarely is that same level of criticism given to Capitalism.

Let me be clear; I do not believe there is anything inherently evil about wealth. I do not believe wealthy people are immoral or evil by default. I believe the conditions in which we live

[46] Marx, Karl. "A Contribution to the Critique of Hegel's Philosophy of Right." Edited by Andy Blunden and Matthew Carmody, *Marx, A Contribution to the Critique of Hegel's Philosophy of Right 1844*, www.marxists.org/archive/marx/works/1843/critique-hpr/intro.htm.
[47] Marx, Karl. "A Contribution to the Critique of Hegel's Philosophy of Right." Edited by Andy Blunden and Matthew Carmody, *Marx, A Contribution to the Critique of Hegel's Philosophy of Right 1844*, www.marxists.org/archive/marx/works/1843/critique-hpr/intro.htm.

incentivize one to pursue wealth at the expense of the moral good. I believe we live in a society that teaches us the world is ours for the taking if only we are willing to do what is necessary to take it. Unfortunately, what is necessary to have it is the capacity for evil or at least complacency in the face of evil that promotes our interest.

It is hard for me to understand why a Christian would support a system that is, at its core, focused on the good of self despite this being contrary to everything Christ taught his disciples. I can understand why a non-believer would support such a system believing it is the only fair way to ensure merit is rewarded. However, to assume such a system is inherently fair is to believe all men are inherently all good, which I do not. As I said in the first chapter, I believe everyone can do good when convenient and evil when necessary.

When you consider the most appealing trait of the Capitalist model, the promise of unlimited earning potential, it is easy to see how such a system could appeal to one's evil capacity. Whereas one person might be satisfied with earning just enough to live comfortably, another would be seduced by that limitless earning potential. Though they may not be inherently evil, their greed would cause them to do evil.

All of this is assuming every one of us has an equal capacity for both good and evil, which we do not. Again, Capitalism, especially in the corporate workplace, creates an environment in which predatory, manipulative, and arguably psychopathic personalities can not only thrive but be rewarded for their evil tendencies. The following is an excerpt from an article written for *Forbes* by Carly Sime:

"These desirable traits [displayed by toxic individuals] include charm, leadership, clear visions, and management skill. Toxic workers can also be highly complementary and present as high achievers, gogetters, passionate, and committed individuals, but what is missing from that snapshot is the whole picture and the fact that toxic workers are only motivated by their gain, which is often at the cost of others... these individuals can be highly successful in their jobs when they are able to ...use a range of... tactics to manipulate situations and get results. They can work themselves into positions of power and thrive in them with their unwavering goal attainment and success-driven behavior... when it positively impacts the business, they work for. It can even leave them being seen as an asset by some.. .when it's a toxic worker achieving these successes, it... will rarely positively impact those they work with."[48]

Based on this, one could even argue that people seeing their peers succeed as a result of their darker traits would adopt those same traits believing they are necessary for success. This creates an environment in which anti-social personalities are not only rewarded but created. This creates an even more toxic environment.

I have heard and read defenders of this system argue that Capitalism does not foster greed. I have even heard them argue that the reality of growing income inequality, and fewer opportunities for poor, working, and middle-class people to advance beyond their current social caste are myths. I have read that Capitalism does not reward greed, but empathy, it does not

---

[48] Carley Sime, "Why Toxicity Thrives In The Workplace," Forbes (Forbes Magazine, February 22, 2019), https://www.forbes.com/sites/carleysime/2019/02/22/why-toxictythrives-in-the-workplace/)

reward competition but cooperation, it does not incentivize selfishness but altruism.

Frankly, I believe such an argument is both disingenuous and insulting. Capitalism only works as a practical system because of free-market economics, which is based on two key concepts, self-interest and competition. If not for these concepts, there would be no exchange of goods and services because there would be no incentive to do so. If not for one's self-interest, desire to maintain their livelihood, or improve it, there would be no incentive to improve one's service or product compared to competitors. If not for that competition, according to Capitalism, there would be no advances in any field.

According to Capitalist philosophy, in the absence of competition, there is no incentive for progress or improvement. So to assert that cooperation and empathy are what make Capitalism work, is to contradict the very foundation upon which Capitalism is built. Therefore, to imply Capitalism in its most basic form is not built of the idea that people are inherently selfish is asinine. And again, why should a Christian support a system based on selfishness?

I want to emphasize for the final time; I do not believe that Capitalism is meritless. It is an undisputed fact that the Capitalist system catapulted the U.S. to the top of the free world. It is undisputed that Capitalism has accounted for many of us enjoying a level of wealth and comfort unimaginable by those who came before. However, Capitalism on any scale other than individual is a system bound to incentivize exploitation through the greed of the powerful.

Sometimes the simplest method of increasing profit margins is not by improving a product or service, but by cutting overhead as much as what is allowable. A number of corporations have utilized this method by stagnating wages, cutting benefits, dodging the taxman, and even receiving taxpayer funded subsidies just for existing ($92 billion in 2019 compared to $59 billion spent on social welfare programs in the same year).[49] Yes, Capitalism does encourage things like innovation and empathy (in the right context). It can even foster cooperation and altruism, but to what end? The primary, if not sole function of a business and therefore a Capitalist centered economy is to make as much profit as possible. If that business fails to do so, eventually, it loses its purpose and ceases to exist.

So yes, a business will support a charitable cause if it helps its image. Yes, it will innovate if a competitor threatens to cut into its profits if not eliminate them. And yes, it will cooperate with other businesses if the merger will help it reach its end goal. Yes, a savvy professional will practice empathy to understand and exploit consumer behaviors. A business may even act altruistically if doing so will not interfere with its primary function of making a profit. A business will do these things if it is in the best interests of that business, or at the very least, does not interfere with those interests.

---

[49] Burst, Todd. "The Welfare State No Longer Aids Those in Need, but Instead Provides Money, Tax Incentives..." *Medium*, Medium, 21 Mar. 2019, medium.com/@tsrub88j/the-welfare-state-no-longer-aids-those-in-need-but-instead-provides-money-tax-incentives-7e71c0072334.

What I believe is that the more wealth one acquires or desires to acquire, for that matter, the more difficult it is for them to devote time, effort, and energy to the pursuit of the kingdom of God. I believe that we live in a society that encourages these attitudes and behaviors by promising unlimited earning potential. I believe the most successful and fulfilled Christians are the ones who see wealth not as an end but to the end of kingdom building. Unfortunately, contemporary Christianity does not enforce this mentality.

If you are like me, you have probably been taught that the first sin was pride, specifically Lucifer's pride, which caused him to exalt himself above God and be cast out of heaven along with a third of the angels in heaven (Rev 12:7-9). This pride entered the world and into man and caused man's nature to become overwhelmed with any number of vices, including greed. I believe pride and greed go hand in hand because the more highly one thinks of themselves; the more they are likely to believe they deserve.

We live in a world where enough is never enough, and due to a real or artificial scarcity of resources, men are left to fight among themselves over those scarce resources. It is only in the instance that cooperation will fulfill our self-interest that we see the community's value. It is our nature, Smith argues, to treat each other not as brothers and sisters but to our own end. I believe all people have a certain capacity for selflessness. However, I believe this capacity is discouraged by our country's consumption obsession.

> "The so-called consumer society and the politics of corporate Capitalism have created a second nature of man which ties him libidinally and aggressively to the commodity form. The need for

> possessing, consuming, handling, and constantly renewing the gadgets, devices, instruments, engines, offered to and imposed upon the people, for using these wares even at the danger of one's own destruction, has become a biological "need."[50]

There is a level of admiration and even reverence that we reserve for those who can consume the most in both quantity and quality. That admiration is why many of us desire luxury items to wear, drive, and live in. It's not because of their inherent quality but because of their status as symbols of our ability to consume and, therefore, our status within society. The idea of a casteless America is a lie told to perpetuate the illusion of fairness.

The impracticality of overcoming generational oppression and inequality and the personal and legislative safety nets created for and by the rich, make mobility for the poor and working classes, especially people of color, a herculean task. So long as we can purchase the symbols of such mobility, however, we are placated at least for a moment. We live in a country and a world, for that matter, where the line between a need and a want is so blurred that the two become one.

Many times, the need is not even a material one. Perhaps you do not need the newest gadget or device because the one you have works perfectly fine. Perhaps you do not need the newest designer clothes or handbag. Perhaps you do not even really want it, but what you do need is the status and self-worth these symbols bring. Consider this study on adolescent attitudes toward self and materialism and more importantly how the two are related.

---

[50] Herbert Marcuse, *One-Dimensional Man* (London: Routledge, 2002)

"In a study of ... adolescents ...material[ism]was the major driver in developing positive attitudes toward luxury brands, where young people who endorsed more underdeveloped self [confidence] showed a stronger tendency to want to display consumption behavior and impress others ...[another study indicated] Children from less-affluent... families endeavor to conceal their relative poverty by buying expensive and high status brands ... children report feeling pressure to wear trainers also possessed by their more affluent peers" [51]

In this country, wealth is not only a symbol of status but an indication of one's strength of character. The myth of the American dream finds its roots in the belief that all one needs to be successful is a strong work ethic, resolve, commitment, and maybe just a little luck. Americans strive for these qualities in themselves and admire them in others. The myth of the American Dream is the myth of American equity and opportunity. It is an idea that implies if one fails, it is their own fault and no one else's.

This works as both the basis and justification for social stratification in this country. It stratifies people according to wealth but legitimizes that stratification upon the idea that wealthy people are so because they have earned it and therefore deserve it. The status that comes with it legitimizes the American social hierarchy by determining class structure not according to birth, but according to merit.

---

[51] Stephen M Butler, "The Impact of Advanced Capitalism on WellBeing: An Evidence Based Model," Researchgate, September 14, 2018, https://www.researchgate.net/profile/Stephen_Butler4)

In this society, only those who deserve riches and the status and influence that comes with it will have it, because they have worked for it, they have earned it. They are favored of God as evidenced by their wealth and favored by society as a result of it. For those who do not, it's because either they lack the desire or the ability to be great and therefore deserve their low status. This quote comes from James Truslow Adams, the man who coined the very term:

> The American Dream is that dream of a land where life should be better and richer and fuller for everyone, with opportunity for each according to ability or achievement. It is a difficult dream for the European upper classes to interpret adequately, and too many of us ourselves have grown weary and mistrustful of it. It is not a dream of motor cars and high wages merely, but a dream of social order in which each man and each woman shall be able to attain to the fullest stature of which they are innately capable, and be recognized by others for what they are, regardless of the fortuitous circumstances of birth or position. [42]

Of course, this is not the case practically speaking as many of us work multiple jobs just to keep our heads above water. Again, my purpose is not to critique the application of advanced Capitalism on income inequality. However, it should be obvious living in America today that something is wrong with the distribution of wealth in this country.

Something about this "bootstraps, gumption, and elbow grease" philosophy of upward mobility just doesn't seem to be working the way it should. Or perhaps it's working exactly as it should but that is a question for another book. This is all perpetuated by the illusion of fairness, and the idea that if one is just willing to work hard enough one can be a part of the American elite, eventually.

On Advanced Capitalist Society's Impact on Contemporary Church

Consider this passage from 1 Corinthians "Looking at it one way; you could say, "Anything goes. Because of God's immense generosity and grace, we don't have to dissect and scrutinize every action to see if it will pass muster. But the point is not to just get by. We want to live well, but our foremost efforts should be to help others live well." (1 Cor 10:23-24 MSG)

Or this from the gospel of Luke: "But love ye your enemies, and do good, and lend, hoping for nothing again; and your reward shall be great, and ye shall be the children of the Highest: for he is kind unto the unthankful and to the evil." (Luke 6:35 KJV).

Perhaps even consider this passage from Philippians: "Let nothing be done through selfish ambition or conceit, but in lowliness of mind let each esteem others better than himself. Let each of you look out not only for his own interests, but also for the interests of others. Let this mind be in you, which was also in Christ Jesus." (Phil 2:3-5 NKJV). Or this most definitive scripture concerning how Christians should conduct themselves according to any world system: "And be not conformed to this world: but be ye transformed by the renewing of your mind, that ye may prove what is that good, and acceptable, and perfect, will of God." (Rom 12:2 KJV).

Now considering these factors, ask yourself should Christians support a system that prioritizes, incentives, and that is built on the concept of self-interest? Should Christians support any social hierarchy, let alone one based on the acquisition of earthly goods? Should Christians embrace a system that not only accepts but utilizes greed as a key component for its perpetuation?

Consider the story of the rich young ruler who came to Jesus asking what he must do to enter the kingdom of heaven. Jesus instructed him to go home and sell all he had and follow him. The man left disheartened because of the attachment he had developed for his earthly treasure, and I would even say just as if not, more importantly, the status and influence that came with his wealth. Recall what Jesus says to his disciples after this episode? "And again, I say unto you, It is easier for a camel to go through the eye of a needle, than for a rich man to enter into the kingdom of God"(Matt 19:24).

As I said in the previous chapter, I don't believe wealth, wealth accumulation, or even consumption are inherently evil. The Bible does teach us however, that the love of wealth is the root of all evil (1 Tim 6:10). I believe the love of wealth is an indicator of greed, and I believe greed is an indicator of pride. As I said earlier, traditionally, we accept that pride was the first sin. Pride is what caused Lucifer to chafe at the idea of living in service to God or anyone else.

As a child of God, one must always strive to do that which is morally good, even at the expense of our own secular pursuits. Some, Christians even, would argue the moral good is not always practical. And I say in what sense? Not practical in the sense of self-interests? "Therefore, I say to you, do not worry about your life, what you will eat or what you will drink; nor about your body, what you will put on. Is not life more than food and the body more than clothing? [...] But seek first the kingdom of God and His righteousness, and all these things shall be added to you." (Matt 6:25-33)

Self-interests should never be the driving force in the life of a Christian. A Christian should not use service as a means to fulfill their own end, but a Christian should see service as a means to fulfill their purpose, which is living a life that glorifies God. As discussed in the previous chapter, pride is what caused Lucifer to think himself equal, if not above, God. Pride robbed Lucifer of his ability to serve by robbing him of his humility. Pride causes one to think more highly of themselves than others. Pride causes one to believe they deserve better than their peers by virtue of their inherent "betterness."

Furthermore, a prideful person cannot be a faithful servant because a prideful person cannot embrace equality, let alone submission. Pride is also what justifies the actions of the greedy. One's "betterness" causes them to believe they deserve better in quantity and quality than their peers, so it justifies not only their attitude, but the actions they take to have better. Therefore, a system that incentivizes greed also encourages pride. For prideful people, service is merely a means to an end. They will do whatever is necessary, including feigning humility, to meet that end. Therefore, every hard worker does not do so because of their work ethic.

Not all loyal people are so because of their love for the individual or group they have pledged loyalty. These qualities for an unscrupulous person are merely a means to an end. There are several people like this in every level of organized ministry, from the smallest storefront church to the highest governing body of the largest denomination. But the Lord said to Samuel, "... For the Lord sees not as man sees; for man looks at the outward appearance, but the Lord looks at the heart." (1 Sam 16:7 AMP)

I cannot recall from who or what I heard this quote, but there is a saying that every society remakes God in its own image. If you want to know what a society truly values, look at its religion. When I say religion, I mean the one they practice, not the one the preach. Although this is counter to what the word teaches, the reality is that modern American Christianity is so intertwined with Capitalist principles, that many churches mirror advanced Capitalism's workplaces.

Even in bodies where appointments are made democratically, the candidates often mirror the same traits and tactics as secular politicians. Such is necessary to gain the influence and favor to be in such a position. Just as we do for our secular social hierarchy, we justify the process by falsely assuming every appointee is so because they have earned it.

 Granted, that last part is partly speculative, but my point stands that corporatism has corrupted our spirituality. I've seen and heard enough to know that it happens in the church. As we discussed earlier, one cannot serve God effectively with natural sensibilities being chief because the flesh does not desire spiritual things. Independent ministries are not immune in that they mirror self-employment. For the self-employed, priority number one is attracting and retaining customers.

If there are no customers, then there is no business. Because of this, independent ministries have another challenge: they can be more susceptible to appealing too much to current and potential membership's secular sensibilities for the purpose of retention. Christians must both accept and embrace the fact that they are not meant to blend into mainstream society. When we accept this fact, we can return to a state in which the early church existed. We can reclaim our status as the salt of the earth. This was the hope of Dr. King in 1963:

> "There was a time when the church was very powerful. It was during that period that the early Christians rejoiced when they were deemed worthy to suffer for what they believed. In those days, the church was not merely a thermometer that recorded the ideas and principles of popular opinion; it was the thermostat that transformed the mores of society."[52]

We must embrace a system of mutual submission. We must strive to serve God through genuine service to one another. We should not concern ourselves with what we might receive for our service, aside from the approval and favor of our God. Such a condition can only be achieved when we all begin to display the same humility Christ did, for humility is the inverse of pride.

> "They [scribes and Pharisees] do all their deeds to be seen by men; for they make their phylacteries (tefillin) wide [to make them more conspicuous]... They love the place of distinction and honor at feasts and the best seats in the synagogues...and to be greeted [with respect] in the market places and public forums, and to have people call them Rabbi...One is your Teacher, and you are all [equally] brothers. Do not call anyone on earth [who guides you spiritually] your father; for One is your Father, He who is in heaven. Do not let yourselves be called leaders or teachers; for One is your Leader (Teacher), the Christ. But the greatest among you will be your

[52] Martin L King, ed. Ali B Ali-Dinar, Letter from a Birmingham Jail [King, Jr.] (University of Pennsylvania), accessed April 14, 2020, https://www.africa.upenn.edu/Articles_Gen/Letter_Birmingham.html)

servant. Whoever exalts himself shall be humbled; and whoever humbles himself shall be raised to honor." (Matt 23:5-12 AMP).

We must be committed to stopping unscrupulous people from and, in some cases continuing to corrupt ministry for their own gain. We must not allow them to influence and manipulate the kingdom by standing idly by as they do so. We cannot continue to complain and brood among ourselves and wait for something or someone else to stop the intruders. We must watch as well as pray. We must commit ourselves to preserving and protecting the kingdom of God not only from spiritual but natural forces. We must be active, vocal, and convicted in opposition to anyone or anything that corrupts ministry.

> "Beloved, while I was making every effort to write you about our common salvation, I was compelled to write to you [urgently] appealing that you fight strenuously for [the defense of] the faith which was once for all handed down to the saints... For certain people have crept in unnoticed [just as if they were sneaking in by a side door]. They are ungodly persons whose condemnation was predicted long ago, for they distort the grace of our God into decadence and immoral freedom [viewing it as an opportunity to do whatever they want], and deny and disown our only Master and Lord, Jesus Christ."
> (Jude 3-4)

Most importantly, we must continually examine ourselves to avoid corruption. Our over-emphasis upon prosperity and positivity are a direct result of Capitalism's influence on the Church and the saints. Both are geared toward appealing to one's self-interested nature, and consequently, both overshadow the believer's commission to selfless service. No sermon of Christ teaches self-love. Quite the opposite is true.

Likewise, there is no such teaching of Christ that declares the believer is entitled to wealth and riches just because they are saved. What Christ does teach is the fullness of joy that comes to those who willingly sacrifice self-interest for God's glory and service to others. We cannot allow our peers' actions and attitudes to cause us to waver or give in to corruption. We must continuously present ourselves before God and hold ourselves accountable to each other and our God.

We must be open and receptive to constructive criticism and Godly counsel regardless of our stature, position, or age. We cannot allow our secular interests to corrupt our spiritual being. We cannot allow our desire for wealth, power, prestige, fame, influence, admiration, or validation be the driving force behind our service.

> "Do not love the world or the things in the world. If anyone loves the world, the love of the Father is not in him. For all that is in the world— the lust of the flesh, the lust of the eyes, and the pride of life—is not of the Father but is of the world. And the world is passing away, and the lust of it; but he who does the will of God abides forever." (1John 2:15-17)

We must always ask ourselves as we work to glorify God through service to others what our end goal is. For a child of God, service should not be a means but the end with the means being our personal agency.

> "But if we evaluated and judged ourselves honestly [recognizing our shortcomings and correcting our behavior], we would not be judged. But when we [fall short and] are judged by the Lord, we are disciplined [by undergoing His correction] so that we will not be condemned [to

eternal punishment] along with the world." (1 Cor 11:31-34)

On The Importance of Honoring and Preserving Good Leadership

What I want to make apparent, which may not be so based on all we covered so far, is that I believe good leadership is necessary for the success of any church. I also believe those leaders must be empowered by the congregation to fulfill their assignments. The value of good leadership is hard to measure and perhaps even harder to measure unless you have experienced both good and bad. For the sake of brevity, I will not go into detail regarding the qualifications of good leadership. The books of Timothy and Titus give all the charges and qualifications for every level of leadership.

A very general summarization of leadership responsibilities is preaching and teaching the word, forming and executing a Godly vision for the ministry, interceding for the congregation, counseling those who need, as well as a number of tasks necessary for the function of ministry. This obviously cannot all be done by one or two people and, in some cases, one or two pastors. According to a 2018 Gallup poll, when asked what was their reason for attending a religious service the percentage of people who rated sermons that teach scripture, sermons that connect with my life, and dynamic leadership as a major factor for their attendance were 76%, 75%, and 54% respectively[53]

"[The Author's] interpretation of these results underscores the importance of church leaders. It is not surprising that church

---

[53] Frank Newport, "In U.S., Four in 10 Report Attending Church in Last Week," Gallup.com (Gallup, January 6, 2020), https://news.gallup.com/poll/166613/four-report-attending-churchlast-week.aspx)

attenders say they go to church to obtain personal and spiritual benefits and surcease from sorrow in troubled times. The key question is: Who or what delivers these benefits? Some personal and spiritual dividends certainly arise from the basic experience of simply being in a house of worship and experiencing all that happens during a church service. However, there is little doubt that outstanding church leadership can be a powerful factor in facilitating the degree to which members feel closer to God, learn how to become better people, and get comfort in times of trouble and sorrow."

Therefore, it is important to have competent and righteous leaders in positions of authority. Leadership does not mean the pastor only. Every deacon, every minister, every auxiliary leader, every trustee, every regional, national, and international officer, must be accountable to God by God's people.

With that being said, the laity must do everything in its power to support their leadership. Sometimes we take for granted just how much of a burden spiritual leadership can be. On several occasions, my pastor has told me that what most people do not realize, especially those who covet a pastoring position, is that only 20% of the job is preaching. When you consider all the responsibilities of a pastor, preaching, teaching, counseling, planning, administrative tasks, fundraising, and so on, that estimation is reasonably accurate. Not only that, but the emotional and mental toll of carrying one's own and the burdens of the people can quickly burn someone out. One pastor, Ray Stedman, decided to save a year-end report given to him by one of his Associate Pastors:

"There are all forms of anger, from long-standing resentment and unforgiveness to rebellion, violence, child-beating, mutilating, wife torture, threats against life, murder for hire, and Mafia-related revenge. There are the sexual offenses of rape, incest, sodomy, homosexuality, gang sex and swingers, bestiality, fornication, and the ever-present adultery. There are marital problems of every kind, attempted or contemplated suicide (and an occasional successful suicide), abortions and adoptions. I see many family problems between parents or single parents and children. There are also the addicts of every sort -- alcoholics, drugaholics, foodaholics, workaholics, sexaholics, spendaholics, etc. There are the institutionalized, either coming from or going to a prison, hospital, detox unit, mental facility. There is the psychotic to deal with or the quieter problems of legal, finances, career questions about a specific passage of scripture or those simply wanting to know about [Our Church][54]

There are several troubling statistics related to pastors and mental wellness. According to a Duke University study, the percentage of clergy suffering from some form of depression or anxiety is twice the national average.[55] According to another study, majority of clergy feel, overworked, under compensated, unfulfilled, and as if their constantly fighting depression.

Almost 40% are either divorced or divorcing. 80% believe ministry has negatively impacted their family life. 50% have admitted to using pornography as a coping mechanism, and almost 40% admit to some form of sexually inappropriate behavior. It is no wonder why so many qualified candidates choose not to accept the call or even abandon the call to

[54] Ray Stedman, "Authentic Christianity," RayStedman.org, accessed April 14, 2020, https://www.raystedman.org/)

[55] Kate Rugani, "Clergy More Likely to Suffer From Depression, Anxiety," Duke Today (Duke University , August 27, 2013), https://today.duke.edu/2013/08/clergydepressionnewsrelease) [48] Bill Gaultiere et al., "Pastor Stress Statistics," Soul Shepherding, November 20, 2019, https://www.soulshepherding.org/pastorsunder-stress/)

leadership—therefore laity must honor their leaders with not only spiritual but natural support. Ministry need not be a high-risk low reward affair. Every minister does not need to be rich, but it is imperative we support those who labor among us spiritually, and practically.

> "Now we ask you, brothers and sisters, to appreciate those who diligently work among you [recognize, acknowledge, and respect your leaders], who are in charge over you in the Lord and who give you instruction, and [we ask that you appreciate them and] hold them in the highest esteem in love because of their work [on your behalf]. Live in peace with one another."(1 Thess 5:12-13 AMP)

While we are discussing compensation, let us address the elephant in the room. There is a perception among both believers and non-believers that there is something unethical about a leader, particularly a pastor, who becomes wealthy through ministry. I disagree. Once again, we must consider the context.
If a minister is supported by a wealthy ministry, why shouldn't the ministers themselves be wealthy?

> "The elders who perform their leadership duties well are to be considered worthy of double honor (financial support), especially those who work hard at preaching and teaching [the word of God concerning eternal salvation through Christ]. For the scripture says, "You shall not muzzle the ox while it is treading out the grain [to keep it from eating]," and, "The worker is worthy of his wages [he deserves fair compensation]." (1 Tim 5:17-18 AMP)

The problem arises when ministers become wealthy, at the spiritual or natural expense of the ministry. I would question a wealthy ministry located in an impoverished neighborhood if that ministry does not have a reputation among the neighbors of being a resource to the people. I would also question a wealthy ministry that does not aid its membership when financially distressed. I would also question a ministry that is financially distressed, yet the leader(s) is wealthy despite the sole occupation of the leader(s) being ministry. Otherwise, I have more of an issue with saints who find the means to and have no issue investing in every aspect of their lives except the one that will last forever.

> "But store up for yourselves treasures in heaven, where neither moth nor rust destroys, and where thieves do not break in and steal; for where your treasure is, there your heart [your wishes, your desirs; that on which your life centers] will be also." (Matt 6:20-21 AMP)

I understand every ministry may not be able to support their pastor financially, led alone their entire ministerial staff; I believe this is where the value of larger organized bodies comes into play. I believe the purpose of a national body of like-minded believers should be to support the local churches spiritually and practically that they might do the same for their clergy and laity. Unfortunately, the inverse is true for many national bodies putting an even greater strain on their member churches and pastors.

I believe there needs to be a symbiotic relationship between all parties. One ought not to be wholly dependent upon the other for preservation. What happens when the best or even good candidates who are competent and righteous choose to abandon or turn down leadership positions is a power vacuum in which authoritarian personalities can control and abuse those positions. It is imperative for saints at all levels of authority to be actively engaged in the governing of themselves, to deter such a scenario.

I have tried to establish in this chapter that I support the need for competent and righteous leaders. I have also advocated for the support and empowering of those leaders. I do not believe that those leaders need to be empowered to the extent of authoritarianism, which, unfortunately, is the state of many small and even large churches. Yes, Capitalism and authoritarianism can and do coexist. This is one of the hallmarks of advanced late stage Capitalism.

In lieu of direct control of the people, an oligarchy composed of a handful of very wealthy corporations and individuals use their wealth to influence the decision making and even the election of legislators. Late-stage Capitalism is too big to be self-sufficient, and therefore it depends on government intervention, typically at the expense of the people. This is because these legislators depend largely on contributions, from whom sociologist C. Wright Mills would call the "Power Elite".[56]

Legislators believe these entities are too big to fail. Their fate is intertwined with that of the government because of the government's willful embrace of this bloated economic system's influence. So here we are in a state in which decades of bad leadership have made the country's economy become dependent upon the corporate oligarchy because said class is

---

[56] Bonn, Scott. "Beware of the Power Elite in Society." *Psychology Today*, Sussex Publishers, 7 Aug. 2017, www.psychologytoday.com/us/blog/wicked-deeds/201708/beware-the-power-elite-in-society-0.

the economy. This is in stark contrast to the narrative pushed by legislators and media of small business being our economic backbone. A quick Google search and a little research will prove my point.

Likewise, in many churches, leaders become dependent on a select few, creating an oligarchy within that church that influences the church's governing and operation as a result of familial ties or financial backing. Tithing today is less than what it was during the Great Depression despite, as us finding earlier, weekly attendance being at its lowest during the 30s and early 40s[57].

Only between 10% and 25% of churchgoers tithe, but the most telling thing, and the stat that backs my earlier claim on church oligarchy, is that 51% of the average church's donations come from a mere 15% of its tithers.[58]   It is hard for me to assume that disparity of donations does not influence how and who influences church governance and even who and how appointments are made.

I know we discussed authoritarianism to an extent, but I want to elaborate on it for the purpose of this chapter. An authoritarian government is one with concentrated and centralized power in

---

[57] Costello, Thomas. "37 Church Statistics You Need To Know for 2019." REACHRIGHT, 25 June 2020, reachrightstudios.com/churchstatistics-2019/amp/.
[58] Costello, Thomas. "37 Church Statistics You Need To Know for 2019." REACHRIGHT, 25 June 2020, reachrightstudios.com/churchstatistics-2019/amp/.

the hands of one (autocracy) or a few (oligarchy).[59] Authoritarian governments accomplish this by exercising arbitrary authority irrespective of existing laws and sometimes using that power to change the law to expand the powers of the ruling party. These regimes are also characterized by a very limited or nonexistent political plurality or opposition.

In addition, authoritarian regimes often resort to using propaganda as a means to fulfill their agenda and maintain authority[60] As strange as this may sound, an authoritarian may have the best intentions for the people, but has become convinced they are the only authority competent enough to govern effectively. It is their ineptitude that perpetuates the conditions they seek to resolve[61] Typically, however, authoritarians are self-serving, using the people to realize their own interests. Authoritarians also

---

[59] The Editors of Encyclopaedia Britannica, "Authoritarianism," Encyclopædia Britannica (Encyclopædia Britannica, inc., November 2,

[60] Steve Denning, "Trump And Authoritarian Propaganda," Forbes (Forbes Magazine, November 15, 2016), https://www.forbes.com/sites/stevedenning/2016/11/06/trump-anda uthoritarian-propaganda/#5780d4033e0a)

[61] Rory Carroll and Jonathan Watts, "Castro's Legacy: How the Revolutionary Inspired and Appalled the World," The Guardian (Guardian News and Media, November 26, 2016), https://www.theguardian.com/world/2016/nov/26/fidel-castrolegacy)

seek to control or suppress opposition using propaganda and punitive measures.[62]

Though I do not support authoritarianism, I think it is unfair to dismiss everything done by such a regime as merely a means for self-preservation. Let's go back to Cuba for a moment. Although Cubans are forced to live in an undemocratic, politically oppressive state, where more than half the population lives in poverty, literacy is virtually universal, both education and healthcare are universally accessible and of high quality, and life expectancy is higher than that of the U.S.[63]

Many churches, both traditional and contemporary, are havens for authoritarian personalities. Because most people tend not to have much invested in the actual operation of ministry, it becomes easy for egocentrics to take over and to dominate. Once they are entrenched, their goal is to remain that way for as long as possible. This is how many churches become little kingdoms and the auxiliaries of that church into fiefdoms. This is how some pastors become dictators executing their agenda regardless of and at times at the expense of the people.

This is how other pastors become puppet leaders acting according to the will of the trustees who selected them and not the God who called them. Therefore so many lay people feel as though they have no real voice or opportunity to exercise their

---

[62] Amanda Taub, "The Rise of American Authoritarianism," Vox (Vox, March 1, 2016),
https://www.vox.com/2016/3/1/11127424/trumpauthoritarianism)
[63] Rory Carroll and Jonathan Watts, "Castro's Legacy: How the Revolutionary Inspired and Appalled the World," The Guardian (Guardian News and Media, November 26, 2016),
https://www.theguardian.com/world/2016/nov/26/fidel-castrolegacy)

gifts within the ministry. This is how many saints, including pastors, quickly burn out. This creates a dynamic of misuse by and resentment toward leadership. Most importantly, this is a big reason why people decide or desire to leave a church. Besides, Christ clearing taught against authoritarianism among saints.

> "But Jesus called them to Himself and said, "You know that the rulers of the Gentiles have absolute power and Lord it over them, and their great men exercise authority over them [tyrannizing them]. It is not this way among you, but whoever wishes to become great among you shall be your servant, and whoever wishes to be first among you shall be your [willing and humble] slave; just as the Son of Man did not come to be served, but to serve, and to give His life as a ransom for many [paying the price to set them free from the penalty of sin]." (Matt 20:25-28 AMP)

I know this chapter feels like a change of pace from the rest of this book. Remember, I never advocated for the abolition of secular or religious government. Recalling the purpose of government, we discussed in the first chapter, if it is in the best interest of a people to do so, the government should be preserved. We need our leaders; more accurately, we need righteous leaders to tend God's flock. As I said earlier, saints must be proactive concerning their spiritual wellness and oversee it. If we value good leadership, I believe we must support, follow, and invest in it, lest we run the risk of allowing self-interested ministers to seize their opportunity.

On The Origins Of Capitalist Theology And The Practical Application Of It In The 20th Century

Though Christianity has been misused over centuries for self interested pursuits, this unique breed of American Capitalist Christianity is actually quite young. In fact, Christianity as we know it today is younger than some of our grandparents. This chapter is not meant to be a comprehensive history on the relationship between Capitalism and Christianity. I do believe it's important for the purposes of supporting the arguments presented in this book, to take a brief look at history to corroborate my claims.

No one individual is responsible for the intermingling of Christianity and Capitalism. However, we can highlight a few especially influential figures during the New Deal Era. Obviously, the business magnates and corporatists of the day were none too pleased with FDR's "encroachment upon our American freedoms", namely the freedom of free market economy.[64] Let it be understood that the creation and spread of Capitalist Theology happened on purpose and through the efforts of many named and nameless Capitalists both in and outside of the church. One of these is Abraham Vereide, a Norwegian immigrant and New Deal Era Seattle Methodist minister

---

[64] Kruse, Kevin M., et al. "How Corporate America Invented Christian America." *POLITICO Magazine*, 16 Apr. 2015, www.politico.com/magazine/story/2015/04/corporate-america-invent ed-religious-right-conservative-roosevelt-princeton-117030.

responsible for the creation of the National Prayer Breakfast, and the organization that facilitates it.[65]

In 1935, Vereide felt a call from God to protect Seattle, and by extension the country, from the corrupting influences of "communism", and when I say communism what I really mean is any threat to free market more specifically labor unions:

> The next day he met a friend, a wealthy businessman and former major, and the two men agreed upon a spiritual plan. They enlisted nineteen business executives in a weekly breakfast meeting and together they prayed, convinced that Jesus alone could redeem Seattle and crush the radical unions.[66]

Vereide and his compatriots were convinced that their call was not to minister to the poor and meek, but to the rich and powerful for only they had the means to establish God's kingdom on earth.[67] By 1943, Vereide's vision was coming to pass. He had been invited to Washington by a "Colonel Brindley" and was granted the opportunity to meet with many influential policy makers. This passage is taken from Jeff Sharlet's article Jesus Plus Nothing, who transposed the passage from Vereide's 1961 biography:

---

[65] Sharlet, Jeff, et al. "[Report] Jesus Plus Nothing, by Jeff Sharlet." *Harper's Magazine*, 18 Oct. 2019, harpers.org/archive/2003/03/jesus-plus-nothing/.

[66] Sharlet, Jeff, et al. "[Report] Jesus Plus Nothing, by Jeff Sharlet." *Harper's Magazine*, 18 Oct. 2019, harpers.org/archive/2003/03/jesus-plus-nothing/.

[67] Sharlet, Jeff, et al. "[Report] Jesus Plus Nothing, by Jeff Sharlet." *Harper's Magazine*, 18 Oct. 2019, harpers.org/archive/2003/03/jesus-plus-nothing/.

> The Vice President brought me to the Capitol and counseled with me regarding the programs and plans, and then introduced me to Senator [Ralph Owen] Brewster, who in turn to Senator [Harold Hitz] Burton—then planned further the program [of a prayer breakfast] and enlisted their cooperation. Then to the Supreme Court for visits with some of them ... then back to the Senate, House .... The hand of the Lord is upon me. He is leading.[68]

Interestingly enough it is Vereide, a Capitalist, who desired to establish what many contemporary Christians accuse Socialists of creating. That being, in his words no less, a "new world order" following WWII.[69] In this new world , there would be no place for radical unions and communist sentiment, only the strength and industrious spirit of God ordained Capitalist ideology. In fact, Vereide's "Family" was successful in getting one of their own, Arthur Langlie, elected as mayor of Seattle in 1938 and later as Governor of Washington state.[70] He would not be the only king of Vereide's making.

Vereide's organization, International Christian Leadership, or "The Family" claimed several important conservative figures as members including Senators Strom Thurmond, Don Nichols, and Hugh Everett. By 1953, Vereide's organization would host its first

---

[68] Sharlet, Jeff, et al. "[Report] Jesus Plus Nothing, by Jeff Sharlet." *Harper's Magazine*, 18 Oct. 2019, harpers.org/archive/2003/03/jesus-plus-nothing/.

[69] Sharlet, Jeff, et al. "[Report] Jesus Plus Nothing, by Jeff Sharlet." *Harper's Magazine*, 18 Oct. 2019, harpers.org/archive/2003/03/jesus-plus-nothing/.

[70] Sharlet, Jeff, et al. "[Report] Jesus Plus Nothing, by Jeff Sharlet." *Harper's Magazine*, 18 Oct. 2019, harpers.org/archive/2003/03/jesus-plus-nothing/.

national prayer breakfast where he courted and lobbied policy makers for a conservative domestic agenda.

Representatives of ICL would continue to travel the globe, meet with and counsel heads of state like former Hatian President François "Papa Doc" Duvalier and President of the Philippines Ferdinand Marcos[71] both of whom are remembered as brutally violent and corrupt authoritarians in the ways of God and right wing politics. The Family would continue to influence the election and appointment of conservatives to federal positions and pushed a Capitalistic agenda for decades after Vereide had passed leadership to Doug Coe.[72] It's interesting to me that Vereide, a devout Christian, chose to dismiss the poor in favor of the powerful despite the Bible's commands to treat everyone as equals regardless of social status.

> For if there come unto your assembly a man with a gold ring, in goodly apparel, and there come in also a poor man in vile raiment; And ye have respect to him that weareth the gay clothing, and say unto him, Sit thou here in a good place; and say to the poor, Stand thou there, or sit here under my footstool: Are ye not then partial in yourselves, and are become judges of evil thoughts? Hearken, my beloved brethren, Hath not God chosen the poor of this world rich in faith, and heirs of the kingdom which he hath promised to them that love him? But ye have despised the poor. Do not rich men oppress you, and draw you before the judgment seats? (James 2:2-6 KJV)

---

[71] Sharlet, Jeff, "The Family," Encyclopædia Britannica (Encyclopædia Britannica, inc., March 20, 2020),
[72] Sharlet, Jeff, et al. "[Report] Jesus Plus Nothing, by Jeff Sharlet." *Harper's Magazine*, 18 Oct. 2019, harpers.org/archive/2003/03/jesus-plus-nothing/.

It's clear that though God does not hate the rich, he is very much aware of how rich men who possess little moral fiber can turn to oppression as both a means and end. The intermingling of Christ and Capitalism was a conscious effort by men like Vereide who may have truly believed they were doing God's will but in truth, were protecting their own pursuits using the name of God as validation.

Reading this, you may have the impression that opportunistic businessmen infiltrated the Church and deceived the unwitting saints into adopting Capitalism as canon. Contrarily, while Vereide and his like took the high ground evangelizing the powerful, others preferred the common touch. This passage has been adapted from *One Nation Under God: How Corporate America Invented Christian America* written by Princeton University professor Kevin Kruse:

> [Rev. Jerry] Fifield told the industrialists that *clergymen* would be crucial in regaining the upper hand in their war with Roosevelt. As men of God, ministers could voice the same conservative complaints as business leaders, but without any suspicion that they were motivated solely by self-interest. They could push back against claims, made often by Roosevelt and his allies, that business had somehow sinned and the welfare state was doing God's work. The assembled industrialists gave a rousing amen. "When he had finished," a journalist noted, "rumors report that the [National Association of Manufacturers] applause could be heard in Hoboken."[73]

---

[73] Kruse, Kevin M., et al. "How Corporate America Invented Christian America." *POLITICO Magazine*, 16 Apr. 2015, www.politico.com/magazine/story/2015/04/corporate-america-invented-religious-right-conservative-roosevelt-princeton-117030.

What Corporate America found in Rev. Fifield was a religious check to FDR's big government encroachment upon the free market. Roosevelt had himself utilized religious rhetoric to promote his New Deal policies. According to biographer James MacGregor Burns, Roosevelt was so apt to quote scripture and use biblical allegories that his speeches were "essentially sermons more than statements on policy".[74]

According to Kruse, Fifield began pastoring the First Congregational Church of Los Angeles in 1935[75], coincidentally the same year Abraham Vereide held his first prayer meeting for the rich and powerful in Seattle. Fifield's congregation was composed of the LA elite, millionaires, and businesspeople. Fifield not unlike many popular preachers today, tailored made his ministry to appeal to his congregation assuring them that their wealth was a sign of God's favor on their lives and that it was God's will that they exercise their individual liberty free of government interference.[76]

Not long after arriving in LA, Rev. Fifield founded Spiritual Mobilization, a faith-based organization focused on promoting conservative economic policy with Christian rhetoric. The organization's mission statement which was "to arouse the ministers of all denominations in America to check the trends toward pagan stateism, which would destroy our basic freedom and spiritual ideals."[77] sounded as though it were inspired more by Enlightenment thinkers like Locke and Smith than by Christ. It also asserted that men had "inalienable rights and responsibilities," specifically "the liberty and dignity of the

---

[74] Ibid.
[75] Ibid.
[76] Ibid.
[77] Ibid.

individual, in which freedom of choice, of enterprise and of property is inherent."[78]

In 1938, Fifield solicited the aid of 70,000 ministers around the country asserting that "America's movement toward dictatorship has already eliminated checks and balances in its concentration of powers in our chief executive." And that the Church had a responsibility to combat this threat.[79] Despite his success gaining clout with conservative law makers and clergy alike, Fifield's mission didn't truly take off until he recruited president of Sun Oil, J. Howard Pew Jr.

If Fifield was the heart of Spiritual Mobilization, Pew became the brain. Pew supported the cause, being a conservatively minded business magnate himself, however he believed Fifield's strategy was much too vague to be effective. Pew sought the help of industrialist consultant Alfred Haake who appealed, as all Capitalist do, not to the ministers' sense of civic duty, but to their self-interest:

> The first step would be making ministers realize that they, too, had something to fear from the growth of government. "The religious leaders must be helped to discover that their callings are threatened," Haake argued, by realizing that the "collectivism" of the New Deal, "with the glorification of the state, is really a denial of God."[80]

---

[78] Ibid.

[79] Ibid.

[80] Ibid.

And it worked. By 1947, Spiritual Mobilization had grown from its initial 400 "minister-representatives" to 10,000.[81] With their success, Fifield and Pew in particular, were able to garner moral and financial support from some of the most recognizable brands like GM, Chrysler, National Steel, Firestone, and Gulf Oil.[82] By the early 1950s, Fifield was so emboldened by his success, that he planned to mark the 175th anniversary of the signing of the Declaration of Independence with a national week of celebration called "Freedom Under God".[83]

Of course, the true aim of these festivities was the promotion of conservative economic policy.[84] The organization went so far as to offer cash prizes to ministers who would prepare a sermon on the theme of "Freedom Under God" and deliver it to their congregations on Sunday July 1, 1951, Independence Sunday.[85] The sermons were even broadcast on CBS' national radio network while festivities were held all that week garnering the participation of right leaning celebrities ranging from entertainers like Bing Crosby and Walt Disney, to politicos like Gen. Douglass MacArthur and former President Herbert Hoover.[86] The great irony of Fifield's crusade was that it's lasting impact had the reverse intended effect.

Instead of engendering suspicion and contempt for government in the people, Fifield had succeeded in causing conservative policy makers to adopt his "Freedom Under God" rhetoric, ergo

---

[81] Ibid.
[82] Ibid.
[83] Ibid.
[84] Ibid.
[85] Ibid.
[86] Ibid.

deifying the federal government as the last greatest defender of Christian values so long as it maintained conservative economic and social policy.[87] My guess is that Fifield would have been just as pleased with this outcome.

> The Christian libertarianism that propelled this religious rhetoric into American politics proved short-lived, but its slogans thrived long after it was gone. Ironically, language designed to discredit the federal government was soon used to sanctify it instead. Throughout the 1950s, a new trend of what the Senate chaplain called "under-God consciousness" transformed American political life. In 1953, the first-ever National Prayer Breakfast was convened on the theme of "Government Under God." In 1954, the previously secular Pledge of Allegiance was amended to include the phrase "under God" for the first time, too. A similar slogan, "In God We Trust," spread just as quickly. Congress added it to stamps in 1954 and then to paper money in 1955; in 1956, the phrase became the nation's first official motto.[88]

The same Christian rhetoric and fear-mongering used by men like Vereide , Fifield, Pew, and many others I haven't covered in this chapter, is the same used by conservative politicians today in order to maintain the support of the so-called "religious right". It is also part of the reason conservatives have adopted a theology of "God and country" as opposed to "God only".

In the minds of many, America is "God's country" and as such America, her ideals, and policies, are viewed with the same

---

[87] Ibid.
[88] Ibid.

reference as God himself. This mentality is rooted in American Exceptionalism. It says that America is somehow inherently exceptional and therefore superior to the rest of the world. As such, though God may not be a literal American, he takes special interests in America, her affairs, and her people above all others even his chosen people Israel. The purpose of this chapter was to show that this was no accident.

It's also to make the point that Capitalist Theology is not just a philosophy I've rationalized into being. It is a near century old amalgamation of conservative (or more accurately Neo-liberal) fiscal policy, American Exceptionalism, and Christian rhetoric. As I said earlier, others have documented this history much more thoroughly than I have and I would suggest that those reading this book would do their own investigating.

Capitalism's impact on contemporary Christianity is a reality that doesn't receive the kind of attention or scholarship it deserves. Instead, we point the finger at phantom Marxist conspiracies, all the while playing right into the hands of conservative establishment. The "new world order" is already here and it has been since we allowed Capitalists to convince us it was our solemn duties as saints to uphold conservative ideology and preach Americana as gospel.

I would like to point out that the scriptures explicitly contradict much of conservative fiscal policy. The Mosaic law required that landowners set aside a portion of their land for the poor to glean (Lev 23:22, Deut 24:10). This provision gave the poor direct access to the means of production rather than depending on the charity of the rich. In case you're unaware, this is a hallmark characteristic of Socialism.

Additionally, according to Mosaic law, there were three separate tithes to be given by the Israelite. These were the sacred tithe given to the Levites who essentially functioned as a de facto government of the ancient Hebrews (Num 18:24), the tithe of feasts which functioned much in the way modern social security does except with broader religious significance (Deut 14:22-27), and the poor tithe which was exactly what it sounds like, a means to create a safety net for the poor, orphans, widows, and migrants (Deut 14:28-29). The purpose for these tithes are confirmed by Flavius Josephus, himself a 1st century Roman Jew, in his historical record *Antiquities of the Jews*:

> "In addition to the two tithes which I have already directed you to pay each year, the one for the Levites and the other for the banquets, ye should devote a third every third year to the distribution of such
> things as are lacking to widowed women and orphan children."[89]

Furthermore, at the end of every seven years, Jews were required to forgive all debts among fellow Jews (Deut 15:1) and on the occasion of every 50th year or "Jubilee" not only would debts be forgiven, but slaves and indentured servants, both Jewish and alien, would be released from service and all land was to be returned to its original owner whether it was acquired through sale or debt (Lev 25).

---

[89] Josephus, Flavius. "Jewish Antiquities: Book IV: Chapter Viii." *Loeb Classical Library*,
(www.loebclassics.com/view/josephus-jewish_antiquities/1930/pb_LC L490.117.xml?result=2.) Edited by Jeffrey Henderson

In fact, God explicitly states "Ye shall not therefore oppress one another; but thou shalt fear thy God: for I am the Lord your God." (Lev 25:17 KJV). According to scholars, these provisions served not only a moral, but a practical purpose namely to prevent economic collapse. Regardless, the idea that God is a Capitalist or would look approvingly on a Capitalist system is one created by man's desire to excuse his greed and the exploitation used to appease it. To be a Christian means to align yourself with righteousness even at the expense of your own self-interest. This is the truth that men like Fifield and Vereide failed to see and it is the truth many Capitalist Christians continue to reject.

On Reconciling the Black and White Churches

Let me admonish you readers that this will be the longest chapter, by far, in this book. This is because the Church's complicity in matters of race is extensive and I want to do my best to paint as clear a picture as possible. Recent events have exacerbated this divide, but it was not created over a few short months or even years. There has always been a division between black and white America and by extension the perspective and worship experience of these two bodies (though the argument can be made that even that has been appropriated and commoditized by Capitalist Contemporary Christianity).

To dismiss this reality by asserting that God is colorblind would be to ignore the reality we live in, which is that though God may be color blind, we are not and white America has never behaved as such. Especially in America, race has shaped our nation, and people in ways that must be examined outside the scope of scripture to appreciate the division between these two bodies truly.

American Christianity is an idolatrous and blasphemous gospel that replaces Christ's teachings of self-sacrifice and salvation, with consumption and hyper-nationalistic pride, it serves as validation for the oppression and subjugation of peoples as a means for national and individual consumption. It is a unique sort of Christian Nationalism that is less Christian than it is nationalistic, and even racist.

It is a fact that white supremacists have polluted the gospel with their sensibilities and have used the scriptures to validate their evil thoughts and actions.

Consider the so-called curse of Ham, which claims people of color are doomed to subjugation due to Noah's son looking on his father's drunken nakedness(this despite scripture indicating that Ham's descendants built the first cities and the Tower of Babel itself),[90] or the creation of the Southern Baptist denomination as a defense of white supremacy and slavery. [91]

The legacy of American Christianity is systemic racism and white supremacy despite efforts being made in recent decades to suppress that legacy. As I stated earlier, the American Church has always been opposed to any threat posed to white supremacy. Unfortunately, to gain the approval of mainstream American Christianity, black Christians have often been nearly as adversarial for the sake of acceptance by mainstream Christianity.

American Christianity is less concerned with the promotion of biblical values than the validation of American Exceptionalist/Capitalist pursuits and ideals. Have you ever considered how many Christians, black and white, seem to be fixated upon homosexuality and women's roles in life and the

[90] Lee, Felicia R. "From Noah's Curse to Slavery's Rationale." *The New York Times*, The New York Times, 1 Nov. 2003, www.nytimes.com/2003/11/01/arts/from-noah-s-curse-to-slavery-srationale.html.
[91] Wadsworth, Nancy D. "The Racial Demons That Help Explain Evangelical Support for Trump." *Vox*, Vox, 30 Apr. 2018, www.vox.com/platform/amp/the-bigidea/2018/4/30/17301282/race-evangelicals-trump-support-gersonatlantic-sexism-segregation-south.

Church? Countless books have been written, and even more, sermons have been delivered, entire organizations have been formed based on one or both of these two topics, and yet there are only a handful of scriptures in a book composed of thousands of verses that references either subject.

In fact, the Mosaic law and the entire Old Testament for that matter, has a great deal more to say about treatment of the poor and migrants, than it does about gays. I believe this is largely because, as I've said multiple times, many Christians resort to using scripture as justification for their biases as opposed to guidance for their living. In fact, I find that many who justify their bias with Bible rarely ever pick up and read one. Or else they would've seen all the other things the word has to say that contradicts them.

Unfortunately, homophobia and misogyny have historically been hallmarks of the American experience, or, more specifically, the white American male experience, the same white males who used the scripture as justification for slavery and white supremacy. Consider the rampant xenophobia and jingoism in this country due in part to scriptural declarations of Christ's teaching being the only true path to God. However, Christ never instructed us to treat nonbelievers with contempt or suspicion, Ironically, only those who corrupt the gospel or believers who deny the divinity of Christ are worthy of our contempt(1 John 4:1-6, Matt 7:15-20, 2 Tim 4:3-4). American Christianity is a distortion of Christ's will and, at worse, a mere tool of oppression.

Many, if not all of America's greatest sins, have been explained away with scripture from the slave trade, to imperialist expansion, to segregation,[92] and even today consumption driven advanced Capitalism (this we covered in the previous chapter). American Christianity is a prideful religion. It does not emphasize contrition and repentance as Christ did. It emphasizes self-interest and superiority.

The American God is not the God of true Christianity, but a mere personification of American Exceptionalism. He is selfish, a racist, a misogynist, greedy, insatiable, suspicious of the other, and filled with misplaced pride in himself. This is the truth about American Christianity. It is an ugly, inconvenient truth, but the truth, nonetheless. White Christian America must accept and embrace and repent of this truth in order to foster reconciliation.

White Christian America has, for most of this country's history, been complicit and even active in the oppression of black America and every other minority groups in this country especially Native Americans. Ironic considering how suspicious so called "native born" Americans are of migrants.

White people in this country, whether descendants of slave owners or not, have benefited directly from the systematic oppression of minorities into a second-class status. It cannot be overstated how policy designed to keep whites at an advantage over blacks has decimated black wealth. It also cannot be overstated how the dearth of policy to overturn the impact of those previous policies has perpetuated the second-class citizenry of black Americans.

---

[92] TISBY, JEMAR. *COLOR OF COMPROMISE: the Truth about the American Church's Complicity in Racism*. ZONDERVAN, 2020.

Many white Americans have reacted to black America's call for equality with a mixture of hostility, unease, and defensiveness because black America's oppression is what enables the privilege enjoyed by white Americans. Yes, equality for minorities would mean the end of white America's current way of living, but is that a bad thing? This country's status quo is one in which a disproportionate amount of privilege and opportunity is vested in white (specifically but not exclusively male) Americans and that reality must be dismantled for true reconciliation to take place.

Exactly how such a reality would be dismantled is what white and black America must discuss and agree upon. However, black America must be made whole before any true reconciling can take place. For this to happen, white America must first experience true contrition, that is to say, a Godly sorrowfulness so intense that it causes one grief.

This grief must be of a magnitude that compels white America to confessing its sins against minorities, and yes black people. Those sums are numerous but can simply be summed up as a systematic and concentrated effort to oppress, dehumanize, and exploit black people at just about every opportunity to maintain the balance of power in favor of whites. As I said earlier that oppression does not always have to be active.

The complacency of those saints who were aware of and yet chose not to combat the spiritual and moral wickedness that led to the state of black, brown, and ever shade apart from white people in this country are just as guilty as the perpetrators. That is the truth, and it must be made clear. Let me also make this point clear. The purpose of this truth is not to demonize White Christian America. To the contrary, embracing this truth would serve to mend ties between the black and white community and establish the relations necessary to make the institutional Church great again.

As we are told in Paul's letter to the Galatian believers, there is no division in the body of Christ. The only divisions are those we have made ourselves, but it must be noted that said division was created for a reason. That reason is white America's unwillingness to embrace blacks as their equals. Just as the secular world's laws segregated black and white America, the arrogance of white America separated the black and white saints, and this created the so-called Black Church. Consider this passage from historian Jemar Tisby's *The Color of Compromise*:

> "Richard Allen and…Absalom Jones entered St. George's to worship. Unknowingly, they took seats reserved for white parishoners and this violated the segregated seating arrangements. They knelt to pray but one of the church's trustees soon interrupted them…[after Jones refused to move until finished praying] The white trustees insisted that Jones leave immediately. Another trustee came over to help pull up the black worshipers. The prayer ended, and Allen recalled, "We all went out of the church in a body and they were no more plagued with us in the church"[93]

Allen and Jones' encounter with their racists brethren was not the first, but it was the one that instigated the creation of the African Methodist Episcopal (AME) Church the oldest historically

---

[93] "Understanding Liberty In The Age Of Revolution And Revival." *COLOR OF COMPROMISE: the Truth about the American Church's Complicity in Racism*, by JEMAR TISBY, ZONDERVAN, 2020, pp. 53–54.

black denomination in America.[94] Unfortunately, this is not an isolated instance of white supremacy's divisive effect on the body of Christ.

Anglicans, Presbyterians, Baptists, Methodists, and even Catholics to a much lesser extent, have all experienced some denominational schism over the slavery question, or more accurately, the matter of whether a Christian, let alone a minister, should own slaves.[95] Pentecostalism, a denomination which owes its genesis to a black man, William Seymour, became divided when white southern ministers struggled with reconciling the unifying power of the Holy Ghost with the Jim Crow laws of the South and the racists attitudes of their parishioners. Instead of fighting the status quo, they opted to do what the establishment Church often does in these instances, they folded and capitulated to the zeitgeist of the age and divided what the spirit of God had unified.[96]

The Church's failure to address and absolve racial issues persisted into the 20th century. During the worst period of racially motivated violence in America that saw widespread lynchings and destruction of black owned property, the Ku Klux

---

[94] "Understanding Liberty In The Age Of Revolution And Revival." COLOR OF COMPROMISE: the Truth about the American Church's Complicity in Racism, by JEMAR TISBY, ZONDERVAN, 2020, pp. 54.
[95] "Defending Slavery At The Onset Of The Civil War." COLOR OF COMPROMISE: the Truth about the American Church's Complicity in Racism, by JEMAR TISBY, ZONDERVAN, 2020.

[96] The Holiness-Pentecostal Tradition: Charismatic Movements in the Twentieth Century, by Vinson Synan and Vinson Synan, W.B. Eerdmans Pub. Co., 2000, pp. 154–155.

Klan was reformed in part as defenders of Christianity from foreigners, coloreds, Jews, and Catholics.[97]

During the Civil Rights Era, white Christians were clear in their resistance to racial equality. In light of the *Brown v. Board of Ed* decision made in 1956 that overturned the "separate but equal" precedent set by *Plessy v. Ferguson,* many church leaders like G.T. Gillespie, The then president of Belhaven College, a Christian institution, adopted a "Christian View of Segregation".

This stance argued that the bible never made any clear indication on whether segregation was justified or not. Therefore, it was perfectly just for segregation to persist under the "Natural Law".[98] Others even equated desegregation to service to the devil himself preaching sermons with titles like "God the Original Segregationist".[99]

Titans of evangelicalism like Billy Graham, took a decidedly more moderate but no less complicit approach insisting it was not their duty to preach against the institutional wickedness of

---

[97] Johnson, Daryl. "Hate In God's Name." *Southern Poverty Law Center,* 25 Sept. 2017, www.splcenter.org/20170925/hate-god%E2%80%99s-name.

[98] "Compromising With Racism during the Civil Rights Movement." *COLOR OF COMPROMISE: the Truth about the American Church's Complicity in Racism,* by JEMAR TISBY, ZONDERVAN, 2020, pp. 132–133.

[99] "Compromising With Racism during the Civil Rights Movement." *COLOR OF COMPROMISE: the Truth about the American Church's Complicity in Racism,* by JEMAR TISBY, ZONDERVAN, 2020, pp. 134

systemic racism. Rather, their duty was simply to preach the word of God and nothing more.[100] Graham to his credit did insist upon desegregating his crowds of listeners threatening not to preach to segregated crowds.[101] However, when riots began to break out across America's urban centers, Graham like many of his contemporaries chose to highlight and denounce the symptoms, instead of the cause which was racial injustice.[102] This is no different than the attitude held by many Christian opponents of this generation's calls for racial justice.

When Richard Nixon, with the help of political strategist Kevin Phillips, deployed his infamous "Southern Strategy" a political gambit to convert southern "dixiecrats" to the GOP by appealing to their increasing dismay over the victories won by Civil Rights activists, it was pastors not politicians who led the charge in converting party affiliation.[103]

When the fight over school integration came to a head during the 70s, it was popular televangelists like Pat Robertson and

---

[100] "Compromising With Racism during the Civil Rights Movement." *COLOR OF COMPROMISE: the Truth about the American Church's Complicity in Racism*, by JEMAR TISBY, ZONDERVAN, 2020, pp. 135

[101] "Compromising With Racism during the Civil Rights Movement." *COLOR OF COMPROMISE: the Truth about the American Church's Complicity in Racism*, by JEMAR TISBY, ZONDERVAN, 2020, pp. 134

[102] "Compromising With Racism during the Civil Rights Movement." *COLOR OF COMPROMISE: the Truth about the American Church's Complicity in Racism*, by JEMAR TISBY, ZONDERVAN, 2020, pp. 141.
[103] Ibid.

Jerry Falwell who were at the front of the anti-integration fight.[104] Falwell formed the Moral Majority in 1979 making the school issue the main point of emphasis.[105] When GOP strategists like Lee Atwater struggled to formulate an effective yet inoffensive alternative to the "n-word", they referred to dog whistles like "criminals" and "thugs" in addition to conjuring the old Postbellum "Lost Cause" mythology.

This myth was built on the idea that the South's role in the American Civil War was a necessary defense of the Southern, Christian, way of life from the intrusion of Yankee interlopers.[106] In a sense, there is some accuracy to this myth as the primary characteristic of the Antebellum South was race based chattel slavery, a reality that in modern times has been conveniently left out of Confederate sympathizers' narrative.

Clergy and politicians alike seized upon the opportunity to harness the contempt held by white Southerners disillusioned with the changing social landscape. This passage is from an article written by Chris Ladd, former political contributor to *Forbes*:

> It was religious leaders in the South who solved the puzzle on Republicans' behalf, converting white angst over lost cultural supremacy into a fresh language of piety and "religious liberty." Southern conservatives discovered that they could preserve white nationalism through a proxy fight for Christian Nationalism.

---

[104] Ibid.

[105] Ibid.

[106] "Reconstructing White Supremacy in the Jim Crow Era." *COLOR OF COMPROMISE: the Truth about the American Church's Complicity in Racism*, by JEMAR TISBY, ZONDERVAN, 2020, pp. 94–95.

They came to recognize that a weak, largely empty Republican
grassroots structure in the South was ripe for takeover and
colonization.[107]

Understand, the "religious right" was created on purpose to
preserve and promote white supremacy, not religion. Many will
argue the religious right was formed to uphold family values and
the sanctity of life, but this is also false. The abortion issue
wasn't even a topic of focus in the 70s when the religious right
was formed. Contrarily, many evangelicals, including prominent
pastors and televangelist, were decidedly pro-choice citing the
traditional theological stance that life began at birth not
conception.[108]

Again, this is a truth that must be embraced before true
reconciliation occurs between the Black and White Churches. As
a direct result of white America's racial arrogance and conceit,
both Christ, his disciples, his teachings, and his ministry were all
whitewashed. Christ, who was by all accounts a dark-skinned
woolly haired, middle eastern man, was turned into a
blond-haired blue-eyed Americanized symbol of white moral
superiority and supremacy and was used as a tool to suppress
and placate the black Christian by promising restitution in the
afterlife in exchange for subservience in this one.

For this reason, many blacks dismissed Christianity as "the white
man's religion," and in a sense, they were correct. American
Christianity, the gospel of Americana, is the white man's religion.
This truth will not be embraced by many due to a combination

[107] Ladd, Chris. "Pastors, Not Politicians, Turned Dixie Republican."
Forbes, Forbes Magazine, 22 May 2017.
[108] Ibid.

of pride and indoctrination. I know this because recent study seems to suggest as such.

There is a saying that history repeats itself and according to recent study, this seems to be the case concerning white Christians' and their perception of the black experience. According to a Barna Group study from 2019, the percentage of self-identified Christians who said our country "definitely" has a race problem was 5 percentage points lower than non-believers who said the same (46% compared to 51%).[109]

Barna Group followed up that study in July of 2020 and found that in the wake of the Covid-19 pandemic, the disproportionate effect it's had on black lives and economy, viral videos of police brutality and white vigilante justice against blacks, and demonstrations against systemic racism, self-identified Christians who considered their faith "very important" were more likely to say race was "not at all a problem" than they were in 2019 (19% compared to 11%). Though more Christians were likely to acknowledge the US' history of racial injustice, the number of Christians who say they feel "little" or "no motivation" to address racial injustice has increased from 18% to 28%.[110]

The true believer will embrace the truth regardless of how ugly it is, regardless of how convicting it is. Or perhaps that

---

[109] "White Christians Have Become Even Less Motivated to Address Racial Injustice." *Barna Group*, 14 Sept. 2020, www.barna.com/research/american-christians-race-problem/.

[110] Ibid.

conviction is what compels the believer to seek reconciliation through confession and then restitution. It is not enough to simply confess one's sins, but to truly create a clean slate; the offender must seek to make the offended whole. They must seek to restore that which was lost or damaged as a result of their trespass. The object of this measure is not retribution.

There should be no eye for an eye exchange, nor should there be any empty posturing or demonstration. Simply, white Christians must denounce American Christianity as an idolatrous, false gospel which primary purpose is as a tool of validation for white imperialist and capitalistic pursuits. The White Church must then embrace the gospel as taught and lived by Christ and in doing so, embrace their brothers and sisters of color and use their privilege to actively create a more equal world, and in the process willfully sacrifice their privilege for the sake of creating that state of being described by Christ when denouncing the lordship exercised by the Gentile kings.

With this restoration complete, the process of reconciliation should be completed by the oppressed in the offering of absolution. Absolution is not mere forgiveness, but it is liberation from the guilt and debt of a transgression. It means not only to forgive but also to forget and create a new bond built on this new foundation of trust and respect.

Some will argue that the sins of the White Church are too great in number and magnitude to be forgotten, but perhaps the Black Church should remember its own failure to live the lives of true disciples of Christ. This is the reality of most Christians white, black, and everything in between. We use faith as an excuse when confronted and convicted by the truth.

Generally speaking, the American Church has failed time and time again to salt this earth, to preserve, that is to say, protect it from spiritual corruption, and enhance it, which is to say make it a better place for all God's people to dwell. However, instead of accepting this truth, we deflect to our distorted half-truth. The excuse most saints will give in regard to their failure to pursue social justice is because it contradicts or impedes our mission of soul winning.

Interestingly, it seems saints are only truly "committed" to soul winning when they are challenged to confront spiritual wickedness as it manifests in our secular institutions. If saints who were discouraged from pursuing justice were truly so for winning souls, wouldn't the Church be bursting at the seams with new converts? However, the opposite is true. The number of self-identified Christians has shrank from 77% in 2007 to 65% in 2018[111] and the number of Americans who claim church membership has decreased from 70% in 1991 to 56% by 2019.[112] The Church is both aging and shrinking due to our abandonment of the world's population while simultaneously embracing its institutions, which is the direct opposite of what Christ instructed.

---

[111] "In U.S., Decline of Christianity Continues at Rapid Pace." *Pew Research Center's Religion & Public Life Project*, 9 June 2020, www.pewforum.org/2019/10/17/in-u-s-decline-of-christianity-continu es-at-rapid-pace/.
[112] Jones, Jeffrey M. "U.S. Church Membership Down Sharply in Past Two Decades." *Gallup.com*, Gallup, 1 Sept. 2020, news.gallup.com/poll/248837/church-membership-down-sharply-past-two-decades.aspx.

Tattoos, piercings and many other things are frowned upon because of one or two references in the Mosaic law, which, again, we've been liberated from through the death of Christ as referenced in Romans 8. To my knowledge, homo and bisexuality are explicitly referenced in a handful of scriptures, specifically those recorded in the Mosaic law (Lev 18:22, 20:13) and those dictated in Paul's letter to the Roman Church (1:26-27) and the letter to the Corinthians (1:6-9) and possibly in the story of Sodom and Gomorrah recorded in Genesis 19, though some have argued these passages relate to rape and ritual male prostitution.[113] Even fewer passages speak directly to the role of women in the Church (1 Tim 2:12, 1 Cor 14:33-35) and those passages are much more ambiguous than those regarding homosexuality. In fact, theologians, including N.T. Wright the former Anglican Bishop of Durham, have cited how those passages are often interpreted improperly and out of the context which they were written, specifically saying of 1 Tim 2:12 that it is "the most difficult passage to properly exegete".[114]

However, I have in study found a plethora of passages, in both the Old and New Testament, that directly address social justice and the believers' duty to pursue it. The entire book of Amos is a book of condemnation against ancient Israel because of its failure to uphold social justice for the poor, yet the Church is not to concern itself with such matters. Isaiah, Jeremiah, and Ezekiel make it explicitly clear that the judgement Israel and Judea were

---

[113] Gnuse, Robert K. "Seven Gay Texts: Biblical Passages Used to Condemn Homosexuality - Robert K. Gnuse, 2015." *SAGE Journals*, journals.sagepub.com/doi/full/10.1177/0146107915577097.
[114] Wright, N.T. "The Biblical Basis for Women's Service in the Church." *Priscilla Papers*, vol. 20, no. 4, 2006.

doomed to endure was a result of their embrace of idolatry and oppression of the poor.

All this tells me the Church of today is less like Christ and more like the world's institutions. How is this? Jesus not only taught but lived a life of service to the neediest among him. He fed the hungry, restored the blind and lame, visited the sick, he openly fellowshipped with the most marginalized people of his day like prostitutes, tax collectors, the poor, and yes, women. Jesus even uncovered the moral depravity of racism when he embraced the Samaritan woman at the well despite the long-standing animosity between Samaritans and Jews.

Perhaps most importantly, despite contrary arguments, Christ openly opposed the political factions he deemed unrighteous, namely the Pharisees. According to Flavius Josephus, the Pharisees held considerable political power and influence over the commoners. This was due to their image as the representatives of the common folk and defenders of Jewish identity and Mosaic law.[115] This was in sharp contrast to the Sadducees who were culturally more Greek than Jewish and by Josephus' account, having only the power to sway the rich.[116] It seems that many Christians only seem to assert disengagement from secular institutions when said engagement does not suit their interests or biases.

---

[115] "Antiquities of the Jews - Book XVIII." *Josephus: Antiquities of the Jews, Book XVIII*, penelope.uchicago.edu/josephus/ant-18.html. Josephus, Flavius. "Antiquities of The Jews Book: Book 13 Chapter 10 Section 6." Translated by William Whiston , *No Document Found*, www.perseus.tufts.edu/hopper/text?doc=Perseus%3Atext%3A1999.01 .0146%3Abook.
[116]

Christ's ministry, at its core, is a message to the oppressed, to those who have little or no hope in this life as a result of oppression exercised upon them by whoever is in power. Just as the Pharisees hid their moral and spiritual failures behind their religiosity, so does the modern Church. That is the cold, hard, ugly, inconvenient truth about the Church, and it must be embraced before we can be reconciled with the people of the world, each other, and, most importantly, with God almighty.

On the Importance of Dissent

"We must not confuse dissent with disloyalty. We must always remember that accusation is not proof, and that conviction depends upon evidence and due process of law. We will not walk in fear, one of another. We will not be driven by fear into an age of unreason, if we dig deep in our history and our doctrine, and remember that we are not descended from fearful men — not from men who feared to write, to speak, to associate, and to defend causes that were, for the moment, unpopular"

Edward R. Morrow

Many believers, both laity and clergy, chafe at the idea of dissent. Conformity has become the standard to such a point that a spirit of authoritarianism binds many churches. Many leaders expect to be treated as rulers instead of servants, despite Christ teaching us contrary. This mentality squashes the free exchange of ideas. Many saints have become disinterested, disengaged, and discouraged by the oppressive nature of their ministry. I want to spend this chapter addressing this issue and offering an argument that supports dissent within church.

I think it is important for us to remember that a dissenter is not always a malcontent. When a person truly cares for something, they will express their concern when that thing begins to corrupt. We all need a little tough love every now and then, and the Church is no different.

"For the Lord disciplines and corrects those whom He loves, And He punishes every son whom He receives and welcomes [to His heart]." You must submit to [correction for the purpose of] discipline; God is dealing with you as with sons; for what son is there whom his father does not discipline? Now if you are exempt from correction and without discipline, in which all [of God's children] share, then you are illegitimate children and not sons [at all]." (Heb 12:6-8 AMP)

I believe most people would avoid confrontation when possible, especially confrontation with authority. Societal norms dictate as much. So, when a person feels enough conviction to defy authority, I believe that defiance is worth acknowledging. Some would argue against encouraging dissent because they believe it encourages rebellion, confusion, division, and dissatisfaction. I do not believe dissent causes any of this; instead, it is the suppression of it that does.

Rebellions rarely occur where there is equal representation and consideration of all viewpoints. Rebellion is the child of desperation and frustration. Is it possible there would be no division by denomination if dissent were entertained and encouraged? I am a believer that the smartest people in the world know that they aren't. In other words, they accept that they don't have all the answers and seek consultation from experts.

Those of you who are Church historians will know the greatest schism in the history of the Church came as a result of the religious authority disregarding a contrary opinion. I am speaking of course of the Protestant Reformation. Our Lord was crucified to suppress dissent.

> "So the chief priests and Pharisees convened a council [of the leaders in Israel], and said, "What are we doing? For this man performs many signs (attesting miracles). If we let Him go on like this, everyone will believe in Him, and the Romans will come and take away both our [holy] place (the temple) and our nation." But one of them, Caiaphas, who was the high priest that year [the year

of Christ's crucifixion], said to them, "You know nothing at all! Nor do you understand that it is expedient and politically advantageous for you that one man die for the people, and that the whole nation not perish." (John 11:47-50)

This is a common refrain of authoritarians; the masses are too incompetent or too fickle to know what is best for them. Because of this, authoritarians believe it is not only their duty but their right to do whatever they deem necessary for the greater good often at the expense of the people's freedom. Authoritarians, often use this line of reasoning to maintain the status quo, as was the case in the above passage. I am not a fan of any form of authoritarianism secular or otherwise because it implies a level of elitism that the Bible clearly teaches against.

"There is [now no distinction in regard to salvation] neither Jew nor Greek, there is neither slave nor free, there is neither male nor female; for you [who believe] are all one in Christ Jesus [no one can claim a spiritual superiority]." (Gal 3:28 AMP)

There is no ultimate authority in the Church except God himself; therefore, we are all accountable to him first and then to each other. No one person has all the right answers this is why the Bible tells us "Where there is no [wise, intelligent] guidance, the people fall [and go off course like a ship without a helm], But in the abundance of [wise and godly] counselors there is victory." (Prov 11:14 AMP)

As a leader, one should always seek a dissenting opinion, if for no other reason, to further debate on a topic. It can be tempting to forego such a thing as to avoid a paralysis by analysis, but how can one be sure if they've drawn the best possible conclusion without hearing all sides of the argument? In the absence of dissent, the opinion of one becomes the rule for all.

This is never a recipe for success. I believe most people understand the logic behind such reasoning; however, pride causes one to think themselves infallible. It is a difficult task being a leader, especially when your intentions are truly pure. It's easy; to become skeptical of others' intentions and competence, the greater your responsibility becomes. This is not, however, an excuse to surround oneself with yes men and women.

Dissent is also integral in developing a person's capacity for critical thinking. It's obvious by this point that I am a firm believer in the importance of critical thinking. Critical thinking allows us to make informed fact-based decisions. Many of us were probably raised in households in which dissent was never encouraged if not completely suppressed by our parents. Many of us who are parents practice these parental policies. "Because I said so," "My house, my rules," and the like are so common they're practically universal. You would be surprised to know such an authoritarian environment is not the healthiest for mental development.

> "We found that what a teen learned in handling... disagreements with their parents was exactly what they took into their peer world,'... The teens who learned to be calm and confident and persuasive with their parents acted the same way when they were with their peers... They were able to confidently disagree, saying 'no' when offered alcohol or drugs. In fact, they were 40 percent more likely to say 'no' than kids who didn't argue with their parents.'"[117]

---

[117] Patti Neighmond, "Why A Teen Who Talks Back May Have A Bright Future," NPR (NPR, January 3, 2012), https://www.npr.org/sections/health-shots/2012/01/03/144495483/why-a-teen-who-talks-back-may-havea-bright-future)

This same philosophy applies to God's children as well. You would be surprised by the number of saints who aren't able to hold their own when confronted by nonbelievers concerning their faith. This is largely because many saints have built their faith on rote memorization of church doctrine and scriptures as opposed to the ability to apply those scriptures in a practical manner. Many saints have learned how to ask the right questions but rarely ask real ones for fear of being ostracized.

The freedom to express a contrary opinion fosters a feeling of genuine care and appreciation. It makes one feel that they are valued, like more than merely a cog in a machine. All of God's children must know they have value, as does their opinion. No one should be ashamed or belittled for going against the grain. Too often in the church, we desire and foster an atmosphere of conformity for conformity's sake. This is because saints just don't like being challenged and much less to change. If someone does not do or think as we do, it makes them deviant by default. This discourages both participation and discipleship.

Now I am very much aware of the multitude of scriptures charging us to obey authority and the punishment that comes to us when we fail to do so. I don't believe these passages are declarations of any authorities' arbitrary right to rule. Such a declaration would be contrary to the many passages of scripture commissioning us to combat injustice. We have many passages giving us examples of God's people confronting unrighteous authorities. Shadrach, Meshach, and Abednego defied Nebuchadnezzar and were saved from death for it.

Nathan rebuked David following the latter's infidelity and murder of Uriah. Ezekiel challenged Ahab and his wife Jezebel to a duel between gods in order to denounce their wicked leadership. Even Jesus rebuked the Pharisees, the political representatives of the common people, as an example of empty religiosity and legalism. So to use three or four scriptures out of context to justify arbitrary rule is a fallacy. Now I want you to consider that Black Americans would still be second-class citizens, if not enslaved, without dissent. Without dissent, women would have no right to vote in this country.

Without dissent, there would be no United States of America. In fact, without dissent, there would be no Protestantism. So, I believe for a woman, a minority, an American, or any Protestant Christian to argue against dissent, it would display hypocrisy or an extreme lack of awareness. I believe these passages are a rebuke against rebellion for rebellion's sake. There are agitators in the congregation, and there will always be.

No matter what is done to foster an environment of cooperation, there will always be one at least one person who is impossible to please, even if their wishes are fulfilled. This should not make leadership fearful of encouraging dissent. If anything, it would display to most people a concerted effort to treat all parties equally, which would turn public opinion in favor of leadership. A leader's job is not to please everyone, especially a few, at the expense of all, but to do what is in the best interests of everyone. However, one cannot know what the people's interests are without hearing from the people.

Now the obvious and most divisive purpose for dissent in the church is to hold leadership accountable. Neither leaders nor laity should ever see themselves as infallible. Truthfully, the more influence one has in secular and spiritual authority, the more susceptible one becomes to believing they are infallible. This is partly because of the inherent sense of validation that comes with any form of promotion. It is also partly because of the great number of people seeking to gain favor through flattery and submission. It is in part, truth be told, because of ego. Regardless, we must all be held accountable, leaders in particular because our task is so grave. We cannot take for granted the salvation of our leaders, for they too will have to give an account for their assignment on earth.

> "Obey your [spiritual] leaders and submit to them [recognizing their authority over you], for they are keeping watch over your souls and continually guarding your spiritual welfare as those who will give an account [of their stewardship of you]. Let them do this with joy and not with grief and groans, for this would be of no benefit to you." (Heb 13:17 AMP)

I think it should go without saying that it is in the best interest of the saints to hold leaders accountable to their divine assignment not just for this life, but in the one that comes after death. We should not be afraid to draw attention to a problem, especially if it jeopardizes our or our brothers' salvation. I would even suggest that one of the telltale signs of a corrupted and therefore, imperiled leader is an inability to receive criticism.

Pride causes one to reach such a state, and as the Bible tells us, "Pride goeth before destruction, and a haughty spirit be a fall" (Prv 16:18). Furthermore, a leader should humble themselves constantly in order to receive dissent and apply it constructively to one's assignment and life. This can all be achieved by remembering Christ's teaching of mutual service and submission.

> "You call Me Teacher and Lord, and you are right in doing so, for that is who I am. So if I, the Lord and the Teacher, washed your feet, you ought to wash one another's feet as well. For I gave you [this as] an example, so that you should do [in turn] as I did to you. I assure you and most solemnly say to you, a slave is not greater than his master, nor is one who is sent greater than the one who sent him. If you know these things, you are blessed [happy and favored by God] if you put them into practice [and faithfully do them]."
>
> (John 13:13-17 AMP)

On the Importance of Biblical Self Sufficiency

"Study and do your best to present yourself to God approved, a workman [tested by trial] who has no reason to be ashamed, accurately handling and skillfully teaching the word of truth. But avoid all irreverent babble and godless chatter [with its profane, empty words], for it will lead to further ungodliness" (2 Tim 2:15-16 AMP)

It is of the utmost importance that saints have not only knowledge but an understanding of God's word. Many of us have committed hundreds of verses to memory, but how many of us truly understand what we are reading? It's important for the saints to know not only how to memorize scripture, but how to study and exegete it. Many traditionalists will swear by the KJV bible (which I prefer not to use in study, for reasons I stated earlier) and yet have very little understanding of old English phrases and terminology, but perhaps more importantly, the context in which that translation was created.

They will have a general understanding of the scripture, but due to the language barrier, an inability to grasp it in totality. Many contemporary Christians choose a more modern translation for their study believing the syntax would give them a complete understanding of the passage. This, too, is not enough, as things like historical context cannot be understood by simply looking at the verse in modern phrasing. Even study bibles are limited in effectiveness due to the author's inability to be completely objective when writing commentary. I believe it is important for a saint to develop an ability to analyze scripture critically, to form organic judgments solve both simple and complex issues of faith, in other words to exegete the text.

Study means more than simply reading. It's more than committing text to memory. Knowledge is useless unless one knows how to apply it practically. One should always study with a purpose. Ask yourself what you seek to gain through this study, what you seek to learn. Typically, when we read a text, we read passively, meaning we are expecting the text to tell us all we need to know. We use repetition and memorization to imprint the text into our heads.

 When the time calls for it, we are able to regurgitate it, but are we sure we understand it? In order to be an effective studier, it's important to engage the material. Ask yourselves questions about the text. Who is the writer? Who is their audience? What is the purpose of this text? Does the culture or time period provide any context? What do I hope to learn from this passage? Are there any contemporary sources I can refer to and how do they make a more cohesive narrative? There is always some new thing to discover when studying scripture. Whether you have never picked up a Bible or you've read the entire written word front to back in every translation, never approach the word feeling as though you know all there is to know. One mistake many saints make is relying solely on reading the Bible, and one translation at that, for study.

Some of us are auditory learners; we do much better hearing the text out loud than looking at it on paper. Some of us, are visual, as I am. One of my favorite features in my study Bible is all the charts, maps, illustrations and graphs that serve as a visual representation of what I'm reading. Verbalize the text, listen to yourself recite it out loud. Draw up your graphs and charts of your own. Get into the mind of the characters you study. Ask yourself what David would do in this situation, what would Paul say on this matter, how would Peter retort. Force your mind to engage the text. Set aside time and a quiet space to study with no distractions.

Take your time. I doesn't matter how quickly you can memorize all the books of the Bible in order and the order in which they were written if you can't understand those books' meaning. It does not matter how many verses you're able to regurgitate if you cannot apply them to your daily life. Approach your study objectively. Too often, we simply turn to scripture to justify or enforce an opinion we have already formed.

We will ignore all the context of scripture; we will disregard every other passage that challenges, if not refutes our claim if we can find the one verse that seems to support our idea. This attitude will not increase your knowledge or understanding in any constructive way. Be open-minded and prepared to have your opinions challenged if not refuted. The ability to change one's mind is not a sign of weakness but maturity and wisdom.

Finally, do not be afraid to supplement your biblical knowledge with other resources. As you've noticed, this book is based primarily on scriptural knowledge, but I've backed my arguments with scientific studies, political theory, sociological text, psychology journals, and other resources to form as concise an argument as possible. Saints need to be holistic in their knowledge. Some saints are afraid that their faith will be corrupted by investing too much time in secular knowledge sources. I reject this idea.

These resources are used to supplement, not replace, God's word as your primary source of spiritual knowledge and understanding. Do not be afraid to challenge what you know with new information. In the marketplace of ideas, sound doctrine will endure when novelty fades. "Truthful lips will be established forever, But a lying tongue is [credited] only for a moment." (Proverbs 12:19 AMP)

All saints need to have both knowledge and understanding of the word. This is a charge that should not be left to leadership alone. Many of the issues I have addressed in this book have come as a result of many saints, both laity and clergy, simply neglecting to study sufficiently. The greatest thing to happen to the Church after the Resurrection was mass production. Once the word was available to the public, written in the common tongue, the flood gates were opened. No longer did the masses have to depend upon religious authority for enlightenment. Of course, this proved to be an issue for those authoritarians in the religious order. The more knowledge the people had, the less control the church was able to hold. Saints cannot depend solely on sermons for biblical knowledge.

First, this is another example of passive learning. Sermons are rarely engaging in that the minister rarely asks non-rhetorical questions or engages in discussion during their message. Preaching is a fundamental part of every saint's spiritual growth, but it is not the only one. As much as we depend upon the spoken word for enlightenment, we must remember preachers are not infallible.

As a preacher myself, I try as best I can to preach in an objective manner, but all things are subject to interpretation and opinion. Those of us who are surer of ourselves than others can even make the mistake of preaching opinion as though it were gospel. Even official Church doctrine is based in part on man's interpretation of God's word. There is so much confusion in the contemporary church because of the many conflicting doctrines in existence. This is in large part because of our desire to validate or justify our own opinions and agendas

> "For the time will come when people will not tolerate sound doctrine and accurate instruction [that challenges them with God's truth]; but wanting to have their ears tickled [with something pleasing], they will accumulate for themselves [many] teachers [one after another, chosen] to satisfy their desires and to support the errors they hold, and will turn their ears away from the truth and will wander off into myths and man-made fictions [and will accept the unacceptable]." (2 Tim 4:3-4 AMP)

If you are one of those Christians with a sincere desire to know God's truth, to know God's purpose for your life, to know how to discern false teaching from sound doctrine, you must be a student of the word. The reformers of the Middle Ages established the doctrine of *sola scriptura*, meaning scripture only. They believed scripture was the sole infallible authority for spiritual enlightenment.

While I wouldn't go so far as the reformers, I believe most Christians will agree that scripture is the final authority for believers. Therefore, if a sermon, a Bible study, a commentary, a doctrine, opinion, or any other practice is not supported by scripture, it has no validity. The question is, how does one know if the practice is valid if one does not know and understand the scripture?

> "My people are destroyed for lack of knowledge [of My law, where I reveal My will]. Because you [the priestly nation] have rejected knowledge, I will also reject you from being My priest. Since you have forgotten the law of your God, I will also forget your children." (Hosea 4:6 AMP)

Not only do we suffer as individuals, but we suffer corporately when the saints neglect to study. A private study life is integral to a saints' ability to think critically, and critical thinking is crucial to re-establishing the Church's relevance. We should not be afraid to challenge any word, regardless of the source, that does not align with scripture. We cannot afford to stand aside and allow fellow believers and unbelievers who seek truth be led astray by errant and even outright false teaching. However, in the same way, we cannot accept a word just because it sounds good to our ears, we cannot challenge false teaching based upon our opinion, but upon the scripture.

> "'I know your deeds and your toil, and your patient endurance, and that you cannot tolerate those who are evil, and have tested and critically appraised those who call themselves apostles (special messengers, personally chosen representatives, of Christ), and [in fact] are not, and have found them to be liars and impostors; and [I know that] you [who believe] are enduring patiently and are bearing up for My name's sake, and that you have not grown weary [of being faithful to the truth]." (Rev 2:2-3 AMP)

One should not develop an intimate study life to debate for debate's sake. We cannot fall prey to the desire of proving ourselves knowledgeable or proving another wrong for our own satisfaction

> "...we know that we all have knowledge [concerning this]. Knowledge [alone] makes [people self-righteously] arrogant, but love [that unselfishly seeks the best for others] builds up and encourages others to grow [in wisdom]." (1 Cor 8:1 AMP)

There is a universal truth in the scripture, despite the many conflicting opinions in the church world today. It's important for one to find their voice in the scripture instead of merely parroting everything they have read, heard, or seen. By studying God's word, we develop a more concise and intimate picture of him and ourselves. We discover our gifts in him and how to use those gifts for his glory.

We discover our weaknesses and how best to overcome them. We become the best versions of ourselves when we not only know God's word but how to apply it to our lives. What does the Bible tell me about handling depression? How did Hosea cope with an adulterous spouse? How would Jesus handle this situation? What can I learn from David's failure to resist temptation? Who am I, and what is my purpose in the Lord? These are the scenarios and questions we can conjure when we combine critical thinking and biblical knowledge. This knowledge is not for us only, but for all those seeking the truth in an age where the truth seems to have become subjective.

> So Jesus was saying to the Jews who had believed Him, "If you abide in My word [continually obeying My teachings and living in accordance with them, then] you are truly My disciples. And you will know the truth [regarding salvation], and the truth will set you free [from the penalty of sin]." (John 8:31-32 AMP)

Despite what some may believe, there are people in this world who desire the truth. Many nonbelievers have become jaded to televangelist ministries and traditional church services because in their mind, it all sounds like the same self-help motivational prosperity message over and over again just with a different tone and cadence. People who are hurting, people who are broken are looking for something authentic.

They're looking for something organic, something that did not come from your favorite preacher's newest book didn't come from your church's doctrinal by laws. They are looking for the kind of truth that can only come from someone who has been in God's very presence. They are looking for the kind of truth that comes from a personal investment into knowing the text and its meaning.

On Spiritual Dependency and Self Sufficiency

"For we [believers will be called to account and] must all appear before the judgment seat of Christ, so that each one may be repaid for what has been done in the body, whether good or bad [that is, each will be held responsible for his actions, purposes, goals, motives—the use or misuse of his time, opportunities and abilities]." (2 Cor 5:10 AMP)

As great a responsibility as spiritual leaders have leading God's flock, our souls' final responsibility lies in our own hands. There is an old aphorism that says you can lead a horse to water, but you can't make it drink. Unfortunately, many saints won't even allow themselves to be led much less drink. Even the most faithful of us will admit that only a small fraction of our time is spent in organized church activities.

Let us assume that a person spends an hour of each weekday in some sort of church activity. Now let us assume that the same person spends between one and three hours in a Sunday worship service. At a minimum, that is 160 hours in a week spent doing something other than church. So much can happen in that time that will challenge one's faith that one simply cannot afford to wait for the next worship service to connect with God.

If truth be told, most of us are far too distracted, willingly in some cases, by the everyday trapping of life to truly devote ourselves to personal growth in Christ. Taking into consideration what we discussed in the previous chapter concerning preachers and opinions, the saints who rely solely on second-hand revelation for growth are more susceptible to false or errant teaching. Because they have not invested time and effort into study, prayer, or fasting, therefore they lack discernment.

Many believers are far too dependent on leadership for growth and enlightenment. You may ask how I can draw such a conclusion. I personally hear far too many believers speak more highly of their leader, their church, or their organization than they do of God himself. They insist upon memorizing and relaying every word that comes from their pastor, or favorite televangelist, or social media prophet and yet rarely do you hear them speak on what God has told them personally or what he has revealed through scripture.

In churches where we believe in and practice the laying on of hands, I see many of the same people coming to the altar every week, many times for the same issues that have no cause other than that person's refusal to take their own spiritual wellbeing seriously. Perhaps most damning is the number of saints who leave the faith when their pastor is caught in a fault.

Instead of building the person back up in Christ, they choose to abandon their faith altogether. Look around your church the next time someone other than the senior pastor is scheduled to preach and count the number of empty seats. Many believers treat the preservation of their faith as more of a chore than a privilege. If there is something you do not want to do, and you know you can pass the responsibility off to someone else, you will. This is largely because we have put far too great an emphasis on the mechanics of worship as opposed to the substance. I believe this is largely due to the explosive growth of Pentecostalism in the last several decades.[118]

Now let me say this before I go any further. I do not believe, nor do I support preaching or teaching against any denomination. I am a Pentecostal myself. I was raised Pentecostal. Therefore, I have witnessed firsthand the two-edged sword that is the Pentecostal explosion. While the number of reported believers has and continues to decrease at an alarming rate, Pentecostals find ourselves representing a greater share of believers than ever before.

> Pentecostalism and related charismatic Christian movements are among the fastest-growing religious denominations in the world. **In** 1980, 6 percent of all global Christians were Pentecostals. By 2015, 25 percent of global Christians were Pentecostal with the greatest concentrations in what's referred to as the "Global South"— largely impoverished regions in Africa, Latin America and Southeast Asia.

This does not even account for the number of mainline and non-denominational ministries that have adopted aspects of Pentecostal theology and worship. Now that last point is the one, I want to focus on for a minute. Traditionally, Pentecostals are some of the most literal adherents to the word.

I grew up in a church where we were told it was a sin for men to have long hair, pierced ears, and even wear shorts or hats to church. Women had it even harder, and we were not allowed to go to the movies or listen to secular music and were discouraged from being friends with nonbelievers. Keep in mind; this was

[118] Dave Roos, "How Pentecostal Churches Took Over the World," HowStuffWorks (HowStuffWorks, June 14, 2019), https://people.howstuffworks.com/pentecostal.htm)

during the mid to late 90s and early 00s. Now the reason I bring this up is because I have noticed many churches adopting a model that has been perfected by many mega and televangelist ministries and that is a form of Pentecostalism that's been appropriated, adapted, and even commoditized to appeal to mainstream sensibilities[119]

I think we Pentecostals must accept a hard truth, and that is that the so-called prosperity gospel finds its roots, at least partially, in Pentecostalism.[120] Pentecostalism is the quintessential holistic denomination. We believe not only in the baptism of the Holy Spirit, but with the Holy Spirit comes several spiritual gifts

"These signs will accompany those who have believed: in My name, they will cast out demons, they will speak in new tongues; they will pick up serpents, and if they drink anything deadly, it will not hurt

---

[119] Stockwell, Stephen, and Ruby Jones . "How Hillsong and Other Pentecostal Megachurches Are Redefining Religion in Australia." ABC News. ABC News, September 26, 2019. https://amp-abc-net-au.cdn.ampproject.org/v/s/amp.abc.net.au/article/11446368?amp_js_v=a3&_gsa=1&usqp=mq331AQFKAG wASA#aoh=15869494901547&csi=1&referrer=https://www.goo gle.com&_tf=From %1$s&share=https://www.abc.net.au/news/2019-08-28/pentec ostal-megachurches-are-redefining-australian-religion/11446368 .

[120] Catherine Bowler, "Blessed: A History of the American Prosperity Gospel," Duke University , 2010, https://dukespace.lib.duke.edu/dspace/bitstream/handle/10161/229 7/D_Bowler_Catherine_a_201005.pdf)

them; they will lay hands on the sick, and they will get well." (Mark 16:17-18 AMP)

We interpret scripture on spiritual gifts and divine intervention quite literally, some of us more literal than others. Pentecostalism has also historically been a denomination that appealed to society's poor and outcasts because of it's equitable nature and belief of God's direct intervention in the lives of his people. This is part of the reason for the denomination's explosive growth in Africa[121], and South America.[122]

The reason why Pentecostalism has grown so dramatically while the rest on Christendom seems to be dying is the tangibility of our God. The sick do not have to accept their sickness. The poor do not have to remain poor. The broken-hearted do not have to remain so because our belief is that God not only can but will intervene on our behalf if we only ask.

"And I will do whatever you ask in My name [as My representative], this I will do, so that the Father may be glorified and celebrated in the Son. If you ask Me anything in My name [as My representative], I will do it." (John 14:13-14 AMP)

Traditional Pentecostals have been some of the most ardent opponents of prosperity theology because it is a corruption of

[121] J.Kwabena Asamosh-Gyadu, "God Is Big in Africa: Pentecostal Mega Churches and a Changing Religious Landscape," Taylor & Francis, May 29, 2019,
[122] David Masci, "Why Has Pentecostalism Grown so Dramatically in Latin America?," Pew Research Center (Pew Research Center, November 14, 2014),
https://www.pewresearch.org/facttank/2014/11/14/why-has-pentecostalism-grown-so-dramatically-inlatin-america/)

our teaching. Many prosperity theologians have their roots in the Pentecostal Church[123] Belief net, we oppose it because it promotes a mentality of secular self-interestedness in its followers. Salvation is no longer the end but the means to acquiring whatever natural end one desires.

0 Followers of this doctrine are less concerned with God than they are with using God to improve their mental, emotional, and physical state. If you recall, in the second chapter, we concluded that by encouraging perpetual consumption and the acquisition of the means to do so, capitalist society leaves us too distracted to focus on things that should matter more to us than they do. The same logic applies to prosperity theology and saints of God.

Too many saints are so focused on what God can do for their physical being that it distracts them from preserving their spiritual being and therefore are not spiritually self-sufficient. Yes, we may read all the scripture we can, attend all the services, faithfully pray and tithe, but to what end? Is it in pursuit of God, or is God simply a means to wealth and consumption? This leads to one dimensional Christianity, a purely self-interested experience at the expense of true fellowship with God. Again, this is one of the hallmark characteristics of Capitalist Theology and is used to control and distract the saints.

---

[123] Beliefnet, "Who's Who in Pentecostalism," Beliefnet (Beliefnet Beliefnet is a lifestyle website providing feature editorial content around the topics of inspiration, spirituality, health, wellness, love and family, news and entertainment., June 30, 2016), https://www.beliefnet.com/faiths/christianity/2006/04/whos-who-inp entecostalism.aspx)

Now arguably, the most appealing aspect of Pentecostalism is our worship experience, which ironically enough was once frowned upon by mainline believers. Pentecostal worship experience is very much a full-body one. As I said earlier, we believe in the tangibility of God that he can literally be felt when we reach out to him through prayer, fasting, study of the word, and of course, worship. In our services, we encourage expression. We encourage, if not expect, the clapping and lifting of hands, dancing in the spirit, and so on.

Our expectation is that through worship, one will feel God's presence and what is felt by the spirit will be expressed by the physical body. So much so is this our belief that many have erroneously developed a process of quantifying spiritual impact by observing the intensity of our physical expression. So much is this concept ingrained in our minds that many ministers preach, teach, and sing to instigate expression colloquially a "praise break."

 This becomes a problem in that many times, we condense if not completely eschew other aspects of our worship services, including the preached word of God, in order to facilitate as much physical expression as possible.[124] This is also becoming a problem in that we develop a habit of ministering (preaching, singing, etc.) In a manner that tantalizes the physical senses in order to elicit the desired response. This creates a self-serving worship experience that some commentators have even

---

[124] Matt Merker and Monique M. Ingalls, "How Contemporary Worship Music Is Shaping Us-for Better or Worse," The Gospel Coalition, February 6, 2019, https://www.thegospelcoalition.org/reviews/singing-congregationcontemporary-worship/)

called "masturbatory."[125]

We have been conditioned to do and say all the right things to illicit and display the desired response, but purely for the response's sake and not the purpose for said response. It creates a condition in which expression is the end goal and not merely a by-product of our experience as it should be. Now, entire ministries are built upon the worship experience's physical expression, leaving their parishioners happily devoid of any spiritual substance.

This combined with contemporary ministries' emphasis of holistic wellness of the individual has created an almost entirely consumer driven church.

Ministries adapt to what the saints demand as opposed to saints changing according to what God requires. This is a direct result of Capitalism's influence on church culture. Black Americans have become accustomed to different aspects of their culture being appropriated and then commoditized for mass consumption. Black music, fashion, dance, language, and even religion have all been adapted, some would even say watered down, to appeal to mainstream taste.

Many modern ministers have found success in adopting and adapting the most appealing aspects of black worship and

---

[125] Jonathan Aigner, "Masturbatory Worship and the Contemporary Church," Ponder Anew (Patheos Explore the world's faith through different perspectives on religion and spirituality! Patheos has the views of the prevalent religions and spiritualities of the world., January 30,2019).https://www.patheos.com/blogs/ponderanew/2019/01/23/masturbatory-worship-contemporary-church/)

marketing them for consumption. So called "shout music" has become ubiquitous to the extent that records are being sold and concerts are being performed that consists almost entirely of said music. Praise breaks, once a spontaneous expression of worship, are now the expected climax of many church services, turning them into performances.

These things are used now to market our ministries as being more appealing than the next and the fish bite. As stated earlier, when these canned praise breaks are paired with the so called "practicality" or "positivity" gospel which eschews selfless service, as Christ taught, in favor of self-love, it creates a church in wish the god of self is the chief deity. Let me be clear, there is nothing wrong, "sinful", or "secular", about preaching and teaching on relationships, finance, entrepreneurship, sex, and other at one time taboo topics in church. The problem, as I keep saying, is when these things overshadow the Church's commission to soul winning and selfless service. It creates a church defined by consumerism not Christ. And in that sense, Capitalist Theology in a nutshell, is a contemporary Christian worship service.

These developments in contemporary Christianity are a direct result of the adaptation of Pentecostalism to mainstream sensibilities. This version of Pentecostalism is tailored to a self-interested society because it centers around fulfilling our physical needs and desires. Unfortunately, it has boomeranged causing many traditional Pentecostal churches to abandon our belief system's less physically self-interested aspects. Many contemporary Pentecostals and pseudo Pentecostals fail to adopt the less glamorous and self-sacrificing aspects of our faith. Traditional Pentecostals do not wait until Sunday to connect with God.

As I said earlier, we should emphasize the importance of prayer, fasting, and the study of God's word as means not for physical expression but connecting with God. When I was a boy, we believed that the expression that was displayed of Sunday was merely a byproduct of our spiritual pursuit throughout the preceding week. Worship was neither a means or an end but merely a result of our pursuit of spiritual growth and relationship with God.

Yes, we believed God would reward our pursuit of him with physical treasures, but that was not the purpose of our pursuit. Once again, the blessing was merely a by-product of the pursuit. Pentecostals traditionally are taught to be self-sufficient Christians. We are taught not to depend solely on leadership for the cultivation and preservation of our spiritual being. We are taught to seek first the kingdom of God and all its righteousness through all the means I mentioned earlier.

Prayer, fasting, and study are the three pillars upon which every Pentecostal believers' life should be built. We sing a song in the Pentecostal church, one of the verses of which say "when Jesus he died/ the veil was rent in twain/ that separated man from God" in other words, we now have free access to him with or without a priest leading the way.

> Therefore, believers, since we have confidence and full freedom to enter the Holy Place [the place where God dwells] by [means of] the blood of Jesus, by this new and living way which He initiated and opened for us through the veil [as in the Holy of Holies], that is, through His flesh, and since we have a great and wonderful Priest

> [Who rules] over the house of God, let us approach [God] with a true and sincere heart in unqualified assurance of faith, having had our hearts sprinkled clean from an evil conscience and our bodies washed with pure water. (Heb 10:19-22 AMP)

Our failure to impart the importance of self-sufficiency for spiritual growth has resulted in an undue amount of influence and power being vested in leadership. This is partly due to emphasizing aspects of ministry that require a minister to facilitate them, and in part to our de-emphasis of spiritual fulfillment through personal relationship resulting in an overreliance on leadership for that spiritual fulfillment.

Now in the case of a self-interested authoritarian leader, this is a perfect condition. The people have no leverage to challenge a self-interested leader because of their lack of spiritual self-sufficiency and or reliance on the minister to fulfill physical interests. Furthermore, that leader because of their influence now can secure their authority by perpetuating the narrative of their supreme authority on spiritual matters and or purposely distracting the people by continuing to appeal to their physical self-interests. This now brings us back to the condition I described in the first three chapters of this book.

This is the condition in which the people's purpose now becomes the preservation of the church and or its leader regardless of whether that leader or church acts in the interests of its people. This creates a condition in which both dissent and critical thought are suppressed to preserve the Church's unquestioned authority. The church then becomes a self-serving, self-indulgent institution too preoccupied with preserving itself than the improvement of the world in which it exists and therefore becomes irrelevant.

This is all to say, for the Church to return to relevance, people must be empowered through self-sufficiency. This self-sufficiency only comes when we are following the words of Christ as recorded by Matthew. "Seek first the kingdom of God and all its righteousness." We must not make the by-products of salvation the goals of our lives any longer. We must not allow secular self-interestedness to be the driving force behind our pursuit of Christ lest we become as Christ described the Pharisees, whitewashed tombs full of dry, dead bones.

On Doctrine and Discipleship

"But I urge you, believers, by the name of our Lord Jesus Christ, that all of you be in full agreement in what you say, and that there be no divisions or factions among you, but that you be perfectly united in your way of thinking and in your judgment [about matters of the faith]. For I have been informed about you, my brothers and sisters, by those of Chloe's household, that there are quarrels and factions among you. Now I mean this, that each one of you says, "I am [a disciple] of Paul," or "I am [a disciple] of Apollos," or "I am [a disciple] of Cephas (Peter)," or "I am [a disciple] of Christ." Has Christ been divided [into different parts]? Was Paul crucified for you? Or were you baptized into the name of Paul? [Certainly not!]" (1 Cor 1:10-13 AMP)

And yet here we are 2000 years after these instructions were written, more divided than we've ever been. The most obvious and historically impactful division is between Catholics and Protestants, but it doesn't stop there are Roman Catholics, Orthodox, Anglicans, Catholic Lutherans, and others. The divisions among Protestants are even more numerous. This does not even account for the many different organizational bodies within those denominations.

Of course, all these divisions came as a result of doctrinal disputes, some serious and others trivial. In many cases, I would argue that egos played a greater role than any disagreements on dogma, especially in the smallest of splits. This is despite teaching to the contrary, "But avoid foolish and ill-informed and stupid controversies and genealogies and dissensions and quarrels about the Law, for they are unprofitable and useless." (Titus 3:9 AMP)

Doctrinal disputes have created more schisms in the body of Christ than can perhaps be counted. Some practitioners will insist their Church's doctrine is the only true doctrine, and every other is heretical. I don't believe there will ever come the point where the entire body of Christ is united under one church doctrine. It's even harder for me to think that there will only be Pentecostals, only Baptists, or only Catholics, or only one denomination in heaven.

Therefore, I think we must prioritize discipleship over church doctrine. Many of our more traditional denominations place such a heavy emphasis on teaching and enforcing doctrine that they neglect simply teaching discipleship. Before we go farther, I want to make a distinction between church doctrine and biblical doctrine.

Every organized body of believers has its own set of values, positions, teachings, and so on that, we refer to as "doctrine." This doctrine is largely based upon that church's governing authorities' interpretation of scripture. Some churches have very loose and broad doctrine, while others quote the opposite. I will give an example of a doctrinal dispute within my denomination of Pentecostalism. I grew up in an organization called Church of Our Lord Jesus Christ (COOLJC), which broke off from Pentecostal Assemblies of the World (PAW).

This split came in part due to a doctrinal dispute concerning the ordination of female ministers. Disputes over things like marriage and divorce, the nature of the Godhead, the divinity of Christ, speaking of tongues, baptismal procedure, apostolic lineage, even things as trivial as the use of wine during communion have led to splits and have been adopted into the official doctrine of churches to distinguish themselves from others. If I could use an analogy, churches are political parties, and church doctrine is the party platform.

Now, most church doctrines are based primarily on scripture, or at least interpretation thereof, but that doesn't make it biblical doctrine. So what is biblical doctrine? Doctrine, in the purest sense, is simply teaching. Therefore, our doctrine is the teachings of Christ and his apostles. As with all things ancient, we must consider both the historical and cultural context when determining what is and is not a biblical doctrine. For example, Philemon is a letter from the Apostle Paul imploring a Christian slave owner (the eponymous Philemon) to accept a runaway slave back into his home as not only his slave but his brother in Christ. Never in the letter does Paul formerly or explicitly request or command for Onesimus (the slave) to be freed.

It's unlikely Paul would have condemned the institution of slavery itself because, at that time, slavery was so culturally and economically ingrained; it was unfathomable to make such a declaration. This is just one example of many I can use to argue the importance of context when it comes to scripture, but I digress. Just because this letter is recorded in the scripture doesn't make it doctrine.

If so, black people would have no right to be emancipated. I believe biblical doctrine is composed of both the requirements of salvation and teachings on the preservation of salvation. So we must ask ourselves, what does the Bible say concerning salvation? From this, we can determine what is biblical doctrine. So the doctrine of salvation can be summed up as thus:

1) Jesus Christ is the son of God sent to take away the sins of the world (John 3:16)

2) He was crucified for the remission of our sins and reconciliation with God being himself (Rom 8:3)

3) He was raised from the dead by the might of his own power. (1 Pet 1:3)

4) One must accept and confess these truths in order to be saved. (Rom 10:9-10)

5) In addition to a verbal confession of faith, one must repent of their sin and be baptized in both water and the spirit of God which is the Holy Spirit (Holy Ghost as it is colloquially known). (John 3:5, Acts 2:38)

Some churches' stance on salvation is a little more involved than this, but it's concise enough to summarize what should be universal to all Christians. Either Jesus or the Apostles taught all that I've stated above as essential for salvation and therefore it's undebatable.

I believe that aside from this, there is no definitive doctrine. When you remember doctrine in the purest and oldest sense of the word, is simply teaching or instruction. It's not a static set of laws or rules. So when Paul refers to "sound doctrine" and men no longer tolerating it (2 Tim 4:3), he is not referencing one monolithic list of rules and laws for saints to live by, but he is talking about well-grounded or well-reasoned teaching and instruction. So this still doesn't answer the question of what is and is not sound doctrine. In a very general sense, sound doctrine teaches that it will preserve one's salvation through living a Godly lifestyle. So what does that entail?

Paul gives the clearest explanation we can find in Titus's 2nd and 3rd chapters (which you can reference at your leisure). Still, even this must be read and understood in context as he refers to slaves to be subject to their masters and charges the women to be homemakers and nothing more. As simple as I've tried to make this, you see how dabbling into specifics muddies the waters. So it suffices to say that all sound doctrine is teaching that will lead one to live in a Christ-like manner.

I believe the confusion lies in human nature. Paul put forth to Timothy that men and women will live how they please and try to justify it with wrong teaching. To prevent this, some leaders have tried to define holiness so strict and precise that to live unholy would be to do so willfully. I wanted to make this distinction between biblical and church doctrine because Christians will bicker because they've reached an impasse on a matter upon which both parties have scriptural basis for their positions and instead of simply agreeing to disagree they declare each other in error when the truth is neither one is.

Now let's define the difference between a member and a disciple. A member is simply a part of a greater whole. One can be a member of an organization, a family, a community, a society, a church, etc. Members will do what's necessary to maintain membership, whether that's paying dues, adherence to laws, or fulfilling any other institutional obligation. Members do what they are charged to do because it's required and expected by the body. When one fails to meet their body's expectations, they run the risk of removal.

On the other hand, a disciple is a follower of a person or that person's teachings the word Christian is anglicized from the word *Christianos* which can be understood as "Christ follower" or more accurately "follower of the anointed one". Notice that Christ's disciples followed him both figuratively and literally. They did this because their faith in him told them wherever he was, was where they needed to be. The more time the spent with Christ, the more they needed him.

It wasn't enough for them to hear one sermon or a few parables. It wasn't enough for them to be given a set of rules and regulations and then sent on their way. Still, they felt compelled to follow him wherever and whenever because there was always some revelation to be had, some lesson to be learned, or some miracle to witness. This is what Christ wants for us, the kind of devotion that comes from spending time with him.

He wants us to have the kind of devotion that comes from personal experience. That devotion creates a desire to share one's experience with others. It also creates a level of authenticity to one's witness that translates to relatability. Simply put, discipleship is devotion. This leads me to conclude that doctrine creates expectations for members to meet, but relationships create disciples who have a personal commitment to Christ. Part of what has made evangelism and retention so difficult for many contemporary churches is our misplaced motives.

Yes, many Christians indeed neglect evangelism altogether, but I believe this has more to do with our motivation why rather than our motivation to do so. We see our churches shrinking, we see our offerings dwindling, so to keep the church from closing, we must motivate lax members to return and nonbelievers to become members. Instead of offering Jesus, we market our churches, the doctrine and why ours is better than the one down the street.

Even if that thought isn't made explicit, we imply that ours is better or more authentic than the next one. What makes this approach to evangelism worse is that once an individual becomes a member, we stop pursuing their soul because our mission has been completed. Now that the person is a part of the congregation, we often leave it to leadership and the church's teachings to lead that person to discipleship. So much is this mentality ingrained in us that many times we find ourselves fishing in someone else's pond.

The overemphasis on doctrine also causes us to create obstacles between the soul and salvation unintentionally. We put ourselves in place of Jesus by insisting this soul can only be saved if they follow whatever rules we do. This discourages and hinders people from seeking Jesus, believing the process is more trouble than it's worth. When the doctrine proves ineffective in soul winning, because it's so ingrained in us that our truth is the definitive one, we make the soul the problem.

We assume people refuse our message because they don't want to be saved or don't want it badly enough. Admittedly, a certain group of people is hostile and antagonistic to believers and the gospel. Still, this group is not nearly as numerous or influential as many of us believe. Truthfully, most nonbelievers are indifferent. They are indifferent because our message is too dogmatic to be relatable and effective.

We must be careful not to exalt our institutions and their platform to a level on par with or above God. This happens when we treat our doctrine as law, creating a state in which saints become more committed to the institution than God. Remember that all church doctrines even biblically-based are the result of human reasoning, and therefore subject to error. Based on this reasoning, to make a commitment to Christ based on doctrine alone is erroneous.

'These people draw near to Me with their mouth, and honor Me with their lips, but their heart is far from Me. And in vain they worship Me, Teaching as doctrines the commandments of men.' (Matt 15:8-9 NKJV)

Remember, our goal should be the salvation of as many souls as possible regardless of which church that soul decides to join. Some have a sincere concern for souls and are wary of objectively false doctrines that may astray people. This is why they are so adamant about instilling their doctrine into a new believer.

Going back to our chapter on knowledge and understanding, rote memorization and regurgitation is not critical thinking. Critical thinking is essential for discernment. One must be able to not only know what is right and what is wrong but also why. One must not only know why something is right or wrong but understand it, comprehend, be able to explain in their own words.

This isn't to say doctrine serves no purpose. It just loses its purpose when we treat it as law. Or rather, its purpose becomes control. Doctrine should not replace relationships as the basis of our commitment to Christ, lest we serve out of institutional obligation and not love for God and his people. It's important to remember good disciples always make good members, but good members are not always good disciples. Good disciples make good witnesses because they can communicate their message from a place of personal experience. Their witness is authentic, relatable, and therefore effective. Even if you're unable to quote one verse of scripture, relaying a personal experience with Jesus is all it takes to create a disciple.

On Community

Humans, by our nature, are self-interested creatures. However, self-interest doesn't necessarily mean solitary. We are social creatures meaning we have a biological need for social interaction. Whether it's in the form of a traditional nuclear family, a multitude of friendships, or even just one intimate relationship, humans crave a sense of community. We are so social; in fact, science suggests young children have an intrinsic desire to help and see others' helped, regardless of any benefit or reward for themselves.[126]

Now, some of you say this fact contradicts the root of my entire argument for the book, that humans are intrinsically self-interested. To the contrary, scientists argue this selfless nature in children is born from our subconscious understanding that two heads are always better than one:

> "the emergence of obligate collaborative foraging in human[s]...provided a new basis for prosocial behavior and helping: interdependence. The basic idea is that when individuals must collaborate or die, their partners become very valuable to them, and so, they must care for them. Within the collaborative activity, this is obvious. If my partner drops his spear, it is in my interest to help him fetch it so that we can continue the collaboration."[127]

[126] Tomasello, Michael. "The Ultra-Social Animal." Wiley Online Library. John Wiley & Sons, Ltd, April 10, 2014. https://onlinelibrary.wiley.com/doi/full/10.1002/ejsp.2015.
[127] Tomasello, Michael. "The Ultra-Social Animal." Wiley Online Library. John Wiley & Sons, Ltd, April 10, 2014. https://onlinelibrary.wiley.com/doi/full/10.1002/ejsp.2015.

The Church, the true Church that is not bound by any doctrinal schism or building, is at its core a family. We greet each other

as brother and sister, not for simple form and fashion but because we are in Christ family. Therefore, a church should seek to foster a sense of community within the congregation. In fact, despite the megachurch explosion of the last two decades, nearly half of all churchgoers, belong to a congregation with no more than 100 members.[128]

Why? Because these churches, theoretically, foster a greater sense of community and belonging. However, we can infer from the precipitous drop in regular attendance that that sense of community has begun to lack. In many congregations, community importance has been corrupted and transformed into its most negative extreme, a sense of tribalism or exclusivity; it has created division and factions within our congregations. If the Church is ever to regain its relevance, we must strive to recapture and maintain the sense of community the early church had. "If a kingdom is divided [split into factions and rebelling] against itself, that kingdom cannot stand. After all " a house is divided against itself, that house cannot stand." (Mark 3:24-25
AMP)

Not only that, but the Church must also seek to be an integral part of the community in which it is located. This can be

---

[128] Peggy Muller et al., "37 Church Statistics You Need To Know for 2019," REACHRIGHT, January 28, 2020, https://reachrightstudios.com/church-statistics-2019/)

accomplished by performing service within and without the congregation. I think that the second point is very important because some of us tend to self-isolate from our neighbors. I believe in the power of pronouns, therefore I try to replace "the"s with "ours", for instance "our community" as opposed to "the community". When we can break down that mental barrier of isolation, inclusion, and the desire to serve our neighbors become much easier. I think we can all agree; it's much easier to serve a beloved family member than a stranger.

> "Then shall the King say unto them on his right hand, Come, ye blessed of my Father, inherit the kingdom prepared for you from the foundation of the world: For I was an hungred, and ye gave me meat: I was thirsty, and ye gave me drink: I was a stranger, and ye took me in: Naked, and ye clothed me: I was sick, and ye visited me: I was in prison, and ye came unto me.   Then shall the righteous answer him, saying, Lord, when saw we thee an hungred, and fed thee? or thirsty, and gave thee drink? When saw we thee a stranger, and took thee in? or naked, and clothed thee?   Or when saw we thee sick, or in prison, and came unto thee?   And the King shall answer and say unto them, Verily I say unto you, Inasmuch as ye have done it unto one of the least of these my brethren, ye have done it unto me."(Matt 25:3440 KJV)

This is the charge on every Christian's life, to serve to poor and downtrodden. If God is a friend to the needy, and we have God in us, then in us should be a desire to help those in need. "If a man say, I love God, and hateth his brother, he is a liar: for he that loveth not his brother whom he hath seen, how can he love God whom he hath not seen?" (1 John 4:20 KJV).

I believe there are three reasons why every church, and every saint, for that matter, should prioritize community service. The first is as a means of evangelism. For all the good we do and hope to do in this world, it would all be for nothing if souls were never saved. "For what will it profit a man if he gains the whole world [wealth, fame, success], but forfeits his soul? Or what will a man give in exchange for his soul? For the Son of Man is going to come in the glory and majesty of His Father with His angels, and then He will repay each one in accordance with what he has done." (Matt 16:26-27 AMP).

 The harsh reality is that most people do not actively seek Christ because most people don't realize how much they need him. What they do know is how hungry they are, how little money they have, how behind they are with utilities. They may not want to be saved at this present time, but what they do desire is someone to visit them in prison, in the hospital and the nursing home. When we display a genuine concern and investment in the physical, emotional, and mental wellbeing of a person, it makes that person more receptive to evangelism.

I see many saints neglect the commission to service because it doesn't meet their end. Service is rarely glamorous. It rarely requires a podium or a microphone, but I believe a service commitment can be more useful for soul-winning than any preached word, especially when it is consistent. I see many churches neglect visitation because the odds of those inmates or nursing home residents joining or even visiting the church are low to nonexistent. I think we can resolve this issue by placing a greater emphasis on the number of souls we escort to heaven than the number of bodies we place in the pews.

Several years ago, our church decided for Martin Luther King Jr. Day, we would volunteer at the local soup kitchen as our act of service. Because she was unable to stand for long periods of time, one of our church mothers wanted to greet the guests as they came in and offer prayer. We were told, understandably so, that we were not allowed to do that because the soup kitchen could not show any religious or political preference.

This was an important lesson for us as a church. We learned that if we wanted to serve both body and soul simultaneously, we would have to do so on our turf on our terms. Let this be a lesson to churches searching for ways to encourage discipleship. Make an effort to be a holistic ministry, and you will find new people flooding your doors not only to be served but to serve. It's incredible how motivated people become to help a church that helps people.

We must also be aware of the state our current members may be in, and be prepared for the saints who have fallen on hard times. Saints who know their church is committed to serving them will be the church's most loyal disciples. I know from experience. When I was around five years old, my mother, a single parent of two, was determined to move my sister and I to a better, safer neighborhood. So much so that she worked two different jobs and cleaned houses on weekends.

I didn't know until a few years ago that she struggled to save enough for a security deposit despite her hard work, and we almost didn't move. So my aunt, her sister, went to our pastor and told him how she struggles to raise the money because she knew her sister was too proud to do so herself. The pastor called her into his office one day after the service was over and asked her to tell him her story. After hearing the story, the pastor asked her one question, "how much?" and the rest was history. I never understood my mother's loyalty to that ministry even after the pastor went on to take his rest until I heard that story.

The second reason I believe churches should prioritize community service is it encourages teamwork. As we said earlier, you'll be surprised at how many people want to contribute. I believe whenever possible, the entire congregation should be encouraged to participate in ministry, especially when that ministry is community-focused. It's very easy for a spectator to become disengaged and feel isolated from the congregation. It then becomes easier for that person to leave the ministry, especially in small churches.

I believe all ideas should be entertained, especially if the idea comes from a faithful laborer in ministry. The thing about most people, especially millennials and zoomers (who we'll discuss at length a little later on), is they don't want to waste their time. So if a church is continuously soliciting assistance in the form of offerings, time, energy, and all of that investment is going in, and nothing or little is going out into the community, it will discourage them from participation. Sometimes the small picture is more important than the bigger one.

Community service also encourages team building and cooperation. It's a sad truth that many churches are struggling with a spirit of internal competition. The competition will only lead to strife and tension, which will discourage others from wanting to be a part.

My final reason why a church should prioritize community service is it is the right thing to do and what God requires.

If we are to live a life that is pleasing to God, if we expect to reap an eternal reward, we must do the will of our heavenly father and love the needy with our words and actions. God has placed in us his spirit and, therefore, his love. That love should cause our hearts to mourn at the suffering of others.

Of course, I believe congregations should donate time to nonprofits and charitable organizations, but should the church itself not be a true sanctuary? There was a time when the church was more than a place of worship but a place of refuge. It was a place where all God's children, believers, and nonbelievers, could come knowing whatever need they had would be met.

As I said earlier, in the Old Testament, there is no shortage of commandments and proverbs concerning the needy's treatment. God cares little for pomp and ceremony when duty is neglected. He will ignore our prayers and please when we ignore those of our neighbors. God promises to reward our service with just rewards, but he also promises judgment to those who neglect it.

> "Then He will say to those on His left, 'Leave Me, you cursed ones, into the eternal fire which has been prepared for the devil and his angels (demons); for I was hungry, and you gave Me nothing to eat; I was thirsty, and you gave Me nothing to drink; I was a stranger, and you did not invite Me in; naked, and you did not clothe Me; sick, and in prison, and you did not visit Me [with help and ministering care].' Then they also [in their turn] will answer, 'Lord, when did we see You hungry, or thirsty, or as a stranger, or naked, or sick, or in prison, and did not minister to You?' Then He will reply to them, 'I assure you and most solemnly say to you, to the extent that you did not do it for one of the least of these [my followers], you did not do it for Me.' Then these [unbelieving people] will go away into eternal (unending) punishment, but those who are righteous and in right standing with God [will go, by His remarkable grace] into eternal (unending) life." (Matt 25:41-46 AMP)

Remember, saints; we are family. We are all God's children. Therefore we have a responsibility to each other. We have a commission to love one another in word and deed. He who doesn't the Bible says is worse than a heretic (1 Tim 5:8). It is impossible for one to claim God's spirit of righteousness and have no urgency to serve their brother in need.

Make yourself sensitive and aware of your brothers' and sisters' needs in the pews and in your community that you may prove yourself a true child of God. Now let's conclude this chapter by saying not all social ills can be cured on the micro-level. There are times in a Christian's life when we must follow our savior's example when he drove the merchants and money changers out of the temple. There are times when we must confront evil directly and forcefully. This is what we will discuss in the next chapter.

On The Church and Social Justice

Let's define what justice is. Simply put, justice is the upholding of what is morally right. According to this logic, social justice is simply what is morally right for society. I know there are many Christians who have become averse to both words and, frankly, the concept. I am here to say, don't be. God is just; therefore, we must be just. We must make it our purpose to do what is morally right. It must be said, as unfortunate as that fact is, that justice is impartial to political affiliation or personal beliefs.

I think we can all agree that the separation of children from their families and the detaining of those children in inhumane conditions is indisputably unjust. I think we can agree, discrimination in any form targeted toward anyone, especially when it results in violence, is unjust. I would even argue unfair labor practices, income Inequality, mass incarceration, and inadequate access to truly affordable healthcare can be considered unjust. Yet many Christians, many church leaders, in fact, turn a blind eye to such atrocities. If fact, many church leaders would insist oppression in this country is a myth. Furthermore, to insist upon such a thing is to distract from the church's purpose:

> "More than 4,700 pastors recently signed a document titled 'For the Sake of Christ and His Church: The Statement on Social Justice and the Gospel.' The document states, 'We reject any teaching that encourages racial groups to view themselves as privileged oppressors or entitled victims of oppression," and "We emphatically deny that lectures on social issues (or activism aimed at reshaping

the wider culture) are as vital to the life and health of the church as the preaching of the gospel and the exposition of Scripture.'"[129]

I find this reality disappointing, but perhaps even worse, I don't find it surprising. The church proper has a history of using scripture to justify bias, which admittedly is the thesis of this entire book. When must we allow ourselves to justify our flesh with the spirit? We must also not fall into the ever-present trap of self-interestedness. I have seen and heard many Black clergies speak and write on various discriminating practices. I have also heard many Latino clergies do the same on immigration issues, but we cannot become so preoccupied with those things that directly affect us that we neglect one another's needs. I'm sure you are familiar with the phrase "injustice anywhere is injustice everywhere," but consider this quote from the man who said it:

> I must confess that I have been gravely disappointed with the white moderate over the past few years. I have almost reached the regrettable conclusion that the Negro's great stumbling block in his stride toward freedom is not the White Citizen's Counciler or the Ku Klux Klanner, but the white moderate, who is more devoted to "order" than to justice; who prefers a negative peace which is the absence of tension to a positive peace which is the presence of justice; who constantly says: "I agree with you in the goal you seek, but I cannot agree with your methods of direct action [...] I have heard numerous southern religious leaders admonish their worshipers to comply with a desegregation decision because it is the law, but I have longed to hear white ministers declare: "Follow this decree because integration is morally right and because the Negro is your brother." In the midst of blatant injustices inflicted upon the Negro, I have watched white churchmen stand on the sideline and

---

[129] Keshia McEntire, "The Church Should Be at the Forefront of the Fight for Social Justice," RELEVANT Magazine, September 12, 2018, https://relevantmagazine.com/current/the-church-should-be-at-thefor efront-of-the-fight-for-social-justice/)

mouth pious irrelevancies and sanctimonious trivialities. In the midst of a mighty struggle to rid our nation of racial and economic injustice, I have heard many ministers say: 'Those are social issues, with which the gospel has no real concern.' And I have watched many churches commit themselves to a completely other-worldly religion which makes a strange, un-Biblical distinction between body and soul, between the sacred and the secular."[130]

I find it disturbing how many Christians will reference scripture to support their opposition to homosexuality, abortion, or even something as universally supported as women's equality. Still, we conveniently omit or ignore scripture that does not support the narrative we're trying to tell. Many will say the Apostle Peter admonished us to submit to both spiritual and secular authority. When you understand the context of the scripture, you will know why Peter says this.

I don't, and I refuse to believe Peter recommended saints submit to immoral and unjust laws because of some arbitrary divine mandate. However, what I do know is the Bible speaks on multiple occasions concerning our commitment to upholding justice. It instructs us to fight in the courts on behalf of those who cannot do so for themselves (Isa 1:17). It implores us to welcome immigrants and refugees, treat them, in the same manner, we do ourselves, and defend them from mistreatment (Lev 13:33-34).

It admonishes us against exploiting the poor and working-class for our own gain (Prv 22:16). To claim institutional justice is not a biblical priority is to prove one's ignorance of or lack of

[130] Martin L King, ed. Ali B Ali-Dinar, Letter from a Birmingham Jail [King, Jr.] (University of Pennsylvania), accessed April 14, 2020, https://www.africa.upenn.edu/Articles_Gen/Letter_Birmingham.html)

reverence for the entire word of God. There are multiple passages in Isaiah and Jeremiah that make reference to "iniquitous decrees" taxing the poor. There are so many references I could use, I would perhaps need to write an entire other book to do them justice.

As we'll discuss at length in the next and final chapter, many churches are bemoaning their inability to retain or reach young people. Because of this, many churches are not only confronted with present irrelevance but a future in which that church no longer exists. Once again, this a disappointing but unsurprising reality. However, the warnings of the old prophets echo in the message of modern Christian soldiers:

> But the judgment of God is upon the church as never before. Suppose today's church does not recapture the sacrificial spirit of the early church. In that case, it will lose its authenticity, forfeit the loyalty of millions, and be dismissed as an irrelevant social club with no meaning for the twentieth century. Every day I meet young people whose disappointment with the church has turned into outright disgust.[131]

What is the greater evil? To commit the crime, or see the crime done and do nothing? I have heard people ask this question many times and have yet to find an answer. I'm also reminded of a quote from one of my favorite movies, "the greatest trick the devil ever pulled was convincing the world he didn't exist."

We dedicated two entire chapters of this book to control through propaganda and distraction. I've avoided as much as

---

[131] Martin L King, ed. Ali B Ali-Dinar, Letter from a Birmingham Jail [King, Jr.] (University of Pennsylvania), accessed April 14, 2020, https://www.africa.upenn.edu/Articles_Gen/Letter_Birmingham.html)

possible mentioning Satan's influence as a cause for our state because I believe we must hold ourselves accountable for our actions or, in this case, lack thereof, and Satan often is an easy scapegoat for the saints. I believe many of us have been deceived into ignoring or, in some cases, justifying injustice so that the church would lose its relevance.

Sincerely I think Satan is always playing for the endgame, and in this case, the endgame is a total lack of impotence by the church. The easiest way to lose your witnessing power is to display hypocrisy. I had a pastor who would always say to the congregation; your actions speak so loudly I don't hear a word your saying. Unfortunately, this is the predicament in which many saints, churches, and organizations find themselves. As some do, I don't believe that a Christian's only means to achieving justice is through sharing the gospel.

Our primary objective as saints of God is always fostering discipleship, but it is not our sole duty. This is a prime example of the one-dimensional pattern of thoughts and behaviors we must break if the church is to become relevant again. As I did in a previous chapter, I would argue a church that shows a commitment holistic ministry has greater witnessing clout than one that doesn't. This should not be the driving force, but it is an incentive.

I must admit that I am perturbed by Christian leaders who imply the pursuit of a just society through confrontation is somehow obtrusive to the sharing of the gospel and salvation of souls. I am equally perturbed by those who imply that those who seek change through conflict neglect to share Christ. At this point in church history majority of saints are distracted from our call to evangelism by a number of things. I don't believe social justice is the one that should give us the most concern. I believe quite the opposite. I believe the church's collective resistance to confronting evil is indicative of our body's moral deterioration, lack of empathy, and spiritual insensitivity.

If anyone says, "I love God," and hates (works against) his [Christian] brother he is a liar; for the one who does not love his brother whom he has seen, cannot love God whom he has not seen. And this commandment we have from Him, that the one who loves God should also [unselfishly] love his brother and seek the best for him. (1 John 4:20-21 AMP)

I do not believe in some arbitrary or divine right to rule bestowed upon government. Yes, the Apostle Peter instructs Christians to submit to both spiritual and secular authority. But understand that Peter was a subject of the Roman Empire, emphasis on Empire. There was no election of officials. Whoever was king or appointed by a king was so regardless of the people's input. The only time a ruler was in danger by cause of the people was if they proved themselves so corrupt or so inept that in caused the people to revolt. Even then, we're talking about the most powerful military in the world going against a rabble of commoners. I know some believe service to the disenfranchised through means other than legislation is enough to change things. I know some believe even if it isn't enough, it is not our place as saints of God to impose upon, or some would even say obstruct the job of legislators (you can refer to chapter one concerning my thought on that).

I like to believe the most intelligent people often find cause to hide their understanding. Therefore, in my opinion, to believe either of these fallacies is to feign ignorance for one's benefit. We must accept, and I believe most of us know that the simple act of giving alms or visiting soup kitchens is not enough to combat certain injustices:

> But the poor person does not exist as an inescapable fact of destiny. His or her existence is not politically neutral, and it is not ethically innocent. The poor are a by-product of the system in which we live and for which we are responsible. Our social and cultural world marginalizes them. They are oppressed, exploited... robbed of the fruit of their labor, and despoiled of their humanity. Hence the poverty of the poor is not a call to generous relief action, but a demand that we go and build a different social order[132]

When a person gives their life to Christ, they commit with their God and their fellow man to serve them both as best they can. I am greatly disappointed with what appears to be a contingency of believers who have chosen to serve their party or even argue their interests and bias over God and man. Regardless of how one may feel about policy and processes, regardless of how one may feel concerning what is and is not lawful, when people are subject to discrimination due to forces outside of their control, it is our duty as agents of heaven in earth to fight such discrimination.

I know many Americans feel that certain groups within and outside of the country as America's enemies or the American way, or American values. Because of this, it's tempting to support an administration that executes policy that combats those enemies. What or who is an enemy, in this case, is

---

[132] Gustavo Gutierrez, *Theology of Liberation* (Place of publication not identified: Scm Press, 2001)

subjective, but for the sake of argument, let's assume they are enemies of the state. The word says this:

> "But I say to you, love [that is, unselfishly seek the best or higher good for] your enemies and pray for those who persecute you, so that you may [show yourselves to] be the children of your Father who is in heaven; for He makes His sun rise on those who are evil and on those who are good, and makes the rain fall on the righteous [those who are morally upright] and the unrighteous [the unrepentant, those who oppose Him]. For if you love [only] those who love you, what reward do you have? Do not even the tax collectors do that? And if you greet only your brothers [wishing them God's blessing and peace], what more [than others] are you doing? Do not even the Gentiles [who do not know the Lord] do that? You, therefore, will be perfect [growing into spiritual maturity both in mind and character, actively integrating godly values into your daily life], as your heavenly Father is perfect. (Matt 5:44-48)

And even still, is a Christian not above all things a citizen of heaven? As citizens of heaven, we must not determine who our enemies are according to any secular government's policy. Unfortunately, this seems to be the modus operandi of American Christianity: the preaching of jingoism as though it were gospel. Additionally, we must embrace and accept that this gospel of Americana is, at its core, nothing more than a tool oppression used for centuries to validate peoples' and nations' subjugation.

Our enemies are God's enemies, the workers of iniquity, the unjust legislators, those who oppress and exploit the poor for their gain, the perpetrators of hateful acts, and any other unrighteousness. Therefore, it is our duty as emissaries of heaven and ambassadors of God's kingdom to represent our king and promote his policy of unconditional love.

As my pastor often says, "love is an action word." If you've ever loved someone, truly love a person as much or more than yourself, there develops inside of you a desire to do whatever is in your power to give this person the best life possible. Christ loved us so much he shed his precious blood that we might be freed from our debt of sin. I think we take for granted the fact that Christ knew the vast majority of those he died for would not accept or even acknowledge his sacrifice.

Many would even deny his very existence. In other words, Christ gave his life not because of some political motivation or ideology. He gave his life, not in the name of a movement or his self-interests. We know he didn't die because he wanted to. In a moment of weakness, Christ begged the Father to relieve him of the task he had been sent to this world to complete it. So why did he do it?

Because his unconditional love for us convinced him it was the righteous thing to do. When one has a love of Christ in their heart, it overrides any bias, prejudice, or agenda and compels them to confront evil and do what is morally just. The very life and ministry of Christ was a confrontation with the religious order of his day. To say it is not the place of a saint to confront unjust authority because it is "God's will" they be so is a logical and biblical fallacy. We must not seek confrontation for confrontation's sake. Still, when legislators have proven themselves incapable of dispensing justice, it is our duty to follow the example of Christ and act in the interest of justice and righteousness.

On the Next Generation of Believers

It's no secret that many churches are having a retention problem. The vast majority of people who grow up in church leave when they become adults.[133] What you may be surprised to learn is that most eventually come back[134] However, this fact doesn't necessarily mean these prodigal sons and daughters return home, so many churches are struggling to survive.

> "Gallup finds the percentage of Americans who report belonging to a church...at an all-time low, averaging 50% in 2018. U.S. church membership was 70% or higher from 1937 through 1976, falling modestly to an average of 68% in the 1970s through the 1990s. The past 20 years have seen an acceleration in the drop-off, with a 20percentage-point decline since 1999 and more than half of that change occurring since the start of the current decade." Jeffrey M. Jones, "U.S. Church Membership Down Sharply in Past Two Decades,"[135]

So the question is, where are all the young Christians going? Since the beginning of the televangelism era in the 1980s, there has been an explosion in mega ministries and mega ministry membership. And yet the number of churchgoers and believers

---

[133] Holly Meyer, "What New LifeWay Research Survey Says about Why Young Adults Are Dropping out of Church," The Tennessean (The Tennessean, January 15, 2019),

[134] Griffin Paul Jackson, "The Top Reasons Young People Drop Out of Church," News & Reporting (Christianity Today, January 16, 2019), https://www.christianitytoday.com/news/2019/january/church-dropout-college-young-adults-hiatus-lifeway-survey.html)

[135] Jeffrey M. Jones, "U.S. Church Membership Down Sharply in Past Two Decades," Gallup.com (Gallup, April 8, 2020), https://news.gallup.com/poll/248837/church-membership-downsharply-past-two-decades.aspx)

has steadily declined since then. Which led many to the following conclusion:

> "'Clearly the majority of the people who came to a megachurch were coming from a congregation nearby. Then there's also a sizable number of folks that say they came to that congregation and they hadn't really gone to any for a long time,' Thumma said. 'If you're moving to a suburb, the megachurch allows you an almost instant community of people who think like you.'" [136]

Now, if you remember a few chapters back, we established that nearly half of all churchgoers (and majority of Protestants) still attend a small church. This is true. It is also true that while mega ministries are growing, the overall number of churchgoers and churches for that matter is decreasing. [137]

This is something that many of us in Christendom have suspected for some time. This is also something we touched on briefly in an earlier chapter. Many of you reading might even be a migrant worshiper, which is not inherently a bad thing. Truth be told, many mega ministries are successful because they offer something many small and medium-sized churches do not. According to one poll, young people count a number of reasons why they choose not to attend a church. Relocation because of work or school is the most prevalent reason, but this was not the only one:

---

[136] Amanda Sakuma, "The Super-Sized Growth behind Megachurches," MSNBC (NBCUniversal News Group, October 24, 2014), http://www.msnbc.com/msnbc/the-super-sized-growth-behindmegac hurches).

[137] Jeffrey M. Jones, "U.S. Church Membership Down Sharply in Past Two Decades," Gallup.com (Gallup, April 8, 2020), https://news.gallup.com/poll/248837/church-membership-downsharp ly-past-two-decades.aspx).

"Seventy-three percent said church or pastor-related reasons led them to leave. Of those, 32 percent said church members seemed judgmental or hypocritical, and 29 percent said they did not feel connected to others who attended. Seventy percent named religious, ethical or political beliefs for dropping out; of those, 25 percent said they disagreed with the church's stance on political or social issues while 22 percent said they were only attending to please someone else. And, 63 percent said student and youth ministry reasons contributed to their decision not to go. Of those, 23 percent said they never connected with students in student ministry and 20 percent said the students seemed judgmental or hypocritical" [138]

Additionally, according to a survey of 1,200 people ranging in ages from 18-24, when asked how much confidence they had in 12 traditional American institutions, organized religion ranked 8th in confidence, just ahead of the federal government and two spots behind the justice system.[139] For the record, only 25% of respondents voice "strong confidence" in the institutional church.[140]

---

[138] Holly Meyer, "What New LifeWay Research Survey Says about Why Young Adults Are Dropping out of Church," The Tennessean (The Tennessean, January 15, 2019), https://www.tennessean.com/story/news/religion/2019/01/15/lifewy-research-survey-says-young-adults-dropping-outchurch/2550997002/)

[139] Crockett, Zachary. "Millennials Have Very Little Confidence in Most Major Institutions." *Vox*, Vox, 28 Sept. 2016, www.vox.com/2016/9/28/13062286/millennials-confidence-in-government.

[140] Crockett, Zachary. "Millennials Have Very Little Confidence in Most Major Institutions." *Vox*, Vox, 28 Sept. 2016, www.vox.com/2016/9/28/13062286/millennials-confidence-in-government.

There isn't much we can do about people moving away. That is their choice and their right. But the other three issues we can surely address and fix. First, I believe we must make a concentrated and sincere effort to meet people where they are. There's an expectation that if someone doesn't instantly change, doesn't instantly begin to act the way we act, speak the way we do, and worship in the same manner we do, they aren't really saved or seeking to do so. My pastor has said many times, "people don't come to church by accident." It's a conscious decision to come to any church, let alone come more than once. Those reasons, if we'll be honest, are not always to seek Christ.

There was a time my sole reason for going to church was because my mother made me. There was a time when my sole reason for coming to church, because I enjoyed playing with the musicians.
There was even a time I would go to a service to meet girls. In all that time, there was always someone who embraced me and loved me where I was. Even when I did begin to become serious about pursuing Christ, I failed many times to meet the standard.

When I did, it wasn't my family I confided in because the guilt of disappointing my mother or sister was too much to bear. Instead, I did confide in someone in the rare instances, it was a church member and not any church member. It was only those who I trusted to both keep my secret and display empathy. Sometimes, a struggling saint needs not to hear another scripture but someone to say, "I've been there." It's not easy to live holy, we must always remember that, and we must also never become so spiritual we lack any earthly good.

Despite popular opinion among traditionalists, I don't believe the reason young people are attracted to large ministries is that these churches have lower standards of holiness, or at least I don't think this is true in all cases. There are small churches with extreme lax standards yet fail to show any signs of growth. So there must be more to the story than that.

 As the quote from earlier in the chapter says, there's a sense of community offered by these larger ministries that unfortunately lack in smaller ones. Perhaps, this is because, with these ministries' largeness, there is less opportunity for personal advancement, therefore less competition among members. It's my personal observation that many small and medium churches suffer from a spirit of tribalism.

It's the same fear and distrust of the other that divides this country, also divides our churches. The prevalence and power of cliques within the church has always been our worst kept and most detrimental secret. These cliques can be composed of many; in such cases, the entire church is one big clique wary of new faces and ideas. These cliques can be composed of a few influential partners bent upon imposing their will upon the ministry.

These cliques can even be composed of one authoritarian personality who doesn't see the value in dissenting opinions. There is almost a cultish devotion to tradition in many churches, and it discourages young people from returning to the churches they grew up in. These cliques discourage the spirit of community and cooperation the Bible teaches us to live by:

> Rejoice with those who rejoice, and weep with those who weep. Be of the same mind toward one another. Do not set your mind on high

things, but associate with the humble. Do not be wise in your own opinion. (Rom 12:15-16 NKJV)

No matter how large or small our church is, we must accept how much we've done as individuals or small groups of such. To help build or sustain that ministry, there must always be a devil's advocate in the room. We must not be resistant to new people or their ideas. I've listened to many people, both young and old, bemoan their respective ministries' repressive nature. Truth be told, according to most, repression doesn't even come directly from the pastor.

Many pastors even feel repressed by certain members of their congregation. As Dr. King described it, I'll admit that the church can feel like an "irrelevant social club" complete with membership fees. There's an expectation that one must submit their agency to the church, or more accurately, to a select few within, to be fully trusted and accepted into ministry. Even if one's name is written on the roll, one is not truly apart until they show a willingness to be a part, a cog in the cliques' machine. We must repress, but embrace and encourage diversity, in gifts, ideas, personalities, and even the worship experience

"For just as the body is one and yet has many parts, and all the parts, though many, form [only] one body, so it is with Christ. For by one [Holy] Spirit we were all baptized into one body, [spiritually transformed—united together] ...God has placed and arranged the parts in the body, each one of them, just as He willed and saw fit [with the best balance of function]. If they all were a single organ, where would [the rest of] the body be? But now [as things really are] there are many parts [different limbs and organs], but a single body... But God has combined the [whole] body, giving greater honor to that part which lacks it, so that there would be no division or discord in the body [that is, lack of adaptation of the parts to each other], but that the parts may have the same concern for one another... Now you [collectively] are Christ's body, and individually [you are] members of it [each with his own special purpose and function]." (1 Cor 12:12-27 AMP)

There's a perception among many elders that young people are generally lazy, entitled, and self-absorbed. On the contrary, many polls and surveys have found that while millennials are less likely to give time or money to a charity, it has more to do with their lack of resources and time than apathy.[141] In fact, many polls and surveys have found that young people value teamwork, activism, and commitment to issues rather than institutions.[84] I think that last point is key in understanding why young people don't see the value in coming to church. As we discussed earlier, an institution's agency comes directly from those who compose it. Therefore, if a church's congregation values activism, the church will value activism.

According to a 10-year study conducted by the Case Foundation, more than 90 percent of millennials said they would stop giving to an organization if they began distrusting it. In a reflection of that trust or lack thereof, more than three-fourths said they would stop giving if they weren't told how their contributions help the cause for which they are giving.[142]

---

[141] Phil & Co, "Why Millennials Aren't Showing up to Volunteer at Your Nonprofit-and How to Get Them There," Phil & Co., January 5, 2017, https://philandcompany.com/how-to-get-millennials-to-volunteer/) [84] Peter Economy, "A New Study of 150,000 Millennials Reveals They Have 10 Surprising Things in Common," Inc.com (Inc., July 27, 2019), https://www.inc.com/peter-economy/a-new-study-of-150000millennials-revealed-that-they-have-these-10-surprising-things-incommon.html)

[142] Peter Economy, "A New Study of 150,000 Millennials Reveals They Have 10 Surprising Things in Common," Inc.com (Inc., July 27, 2019),

Young people consider their time and money valuable enough that they need to be given a reason to expend either. I think we can all agree that Jesus' ministry began to pick up when he proved himself to be not just a teacher, but a miracle worker and a doer of his own word. People flocked to Jesus because he gave them a reason to. I'm convinced, many of Jesus' disciples didn't come to Jesus because he offered salvation, but they came because things he was saying and doing were so authentic.

We must apply that same mentality to our witnessing efforts today. We must show a commitment to the same issues that concern the next generation and do so with sincerity. Of course, we can argue that Jesus is the only reason one needs to attend church, but in a world where many people are convinced they don't need to go to church to have a relationship with Jesus, the church needs to demonstrate to young people the same passion for people as they.

This is especially true considering there is a very vocal contingent of so called evangelicals who do not display the same love that Christ display (I won't go further than in this book than I already have) and unfortunately, because of how vocal and visible they are and how silent we are many people outside of church assume they speak for the entirety of Christendom. Though we know this is false, the unchurched will have no idea unless we speak just as loudly and become visible.

---

https://www.inc.com/peter-economy/a-new-study-of-150000millennia ls-revealed-that-they-have-these-10-surprising-things-incommon.html)

Before we conclude this chapter, let's talk about youth ministry. I believe every church should have a dedicated youth ministry and ministerial workers. As we said earlier, each new generation has different values, and to reach each generation, we must appeal to those values. We've already established young people today have a great passion for issues but not institutions. Therefore, we must expand ministry beyond the four walls of the church.

We must emphasize fellowship over membership. There is a delicate balance between sharing Jesus and allowing people to come to him on their terms. The latter is the key to developing disciples before members. We must show the love of Christ as opposed to the love of church. We must know our audience before we speak, and when we do speak, we must do so in a manner and to things they can relate to. "And I, brethren, when I came to you, came not with excellency of speech or of wisdom, declaring unto you the testimony of God."(1 Cor 2:1 KJV).

Every message does not need to be a sermon. A simple testimony of God's goodness in your life can convert an unbeliever to a disciple. It's hard to reach a generation indifferent to tradition through traditional means, so we must make an effort to think outside the box. We've covered this earlier, but I cannot overemphasize the importance of community service in any ministry, large or small. It plays a tremendous role in shaping a church's image in the minds of the community, membership, and others. How active a church is in its community could very well be what convinces one to join or not join a church.

Finally, I would suggest every church embrace technology. Social media is a good place to begin, but consider creating a website for your ministry and updating it frequently with not only the church's schedule, but church's mission, a bit about the church's history, staff and membership, and finally, activities and causes the church is both spearheading and participating. I see many church websites and websites of international organizations, even with websites that look as if they haven't been updated since the nineties. Make it a point to allow individuals to interact with your ministry online. Perhaps this will be the impetus that moves them from apathy to potentially discipleship.

Final Thoughts

As I've tried to reiterate multiple times, this book is not meant to be a condemnation, but a call to action. Our churches are dying a slow needless death as a result of decades long complacency. I will admit that I was one of those people who had just surrendered to the idea that people just weren't interested in Jesus anymore.

Then I began to read between the lines. I began to actually talk to people, find out what they were thinking. I visited churches that had committed themselves to sharing the gospel through works and words and how successful they were in doing so. That's when I realized, there is still a need and desire for truth in the hearts of people, it's just that many of those people don't believe an organized institution is necessary for that.

When I was a child, I went to a pediatrician who had a painting on the wall of their waiting room. It was small and it looked as if it had been done by a child (this was a pediatrician after all). Drawn in crayon of every color in the rainbow, it was a picture of a house, a car, a few bags of money, and some crudely drawn figures meant to be a family.

The thing that always stuck with me about that picture was a quote written on the bottom right corner of the frame. It said " In a hundred years, it won't matter how big your house was, it won't matter what kind of car you drove, it won't even matter how much money you made. What will matter is the difference you made in the life of a child".

This philosophy is the same one I apply to my personal ministry, and I pray every believer applies to theirs. I've always been taught that the judgement of the saints will be an account for all our Godly works. I've even referenced several scriptures concerning the charge of Christians to show the love of Christ through service. If I could, I would like to end this book with one more.

> "If I do not the works of my Father, believe me not.   But if I do, though ye believe not me, believe the works: that ye may know, and believe, that the Father is in me, and I in him."

(John 10:37-38 KJV)

Although Christ was referring to the miracles he performed, does the same principle not apply to us? What reason would one have to believe I am not a servant if I don't serve anyone but myself? What reason would they have to believe I love them with the love of Christ if I don't do the things to express such love? Why should one believe I am Christian in more than name if I don't do things Christ would do?

I want to be able to live a life with which I can be satisfied knowing when I take my final rest, that I had done all in my power to live like Christ, who was willing to lay down his life even for those who despised him, and left a legacy that made a difference in someone's life. I believe this should be the goal of every Christian.

Our mission is not relevant for the sake of it, but for the purpose of claiming a captive audience for the message of hope and salvation. When the world knows beyond a shadow of a doubt, that the Church cares, we will see the world begin to care about us again. And when that day comes I hope we will all be ready to share the good news with those who will hear it, that one day when we're called to be with Jesus we can hear "well done thou good and faithful servant...enter into the joy of the lord". God Bless you and may heaven smile upon you.

Cited Works

Adams, James T. "The Epic Of America By James Truslow Adams."
Bartleby. Accessed April 14, 2020.
https://www.bartleby.com/essay/The-Epic-Of-America-By-Jame
s-Truslow-P3H7J9VZA4FP.

Aigner, Jonathan. "Masturbatory Worship and the Contemporary
Church." Ponder Anew. Patheos Explore the world's faith
through different perspectives on religion and spirituality!
Patheos has the views of the prevalent religions and
spiritualities of the world., January 30, 2019.
https://www.patheos.com/blogs/ponderanew/2019/01/23/mas
turbatory-worship-contemporary-church/.

Asamosh-Gyadu, J.Kwabena. "God Is Big in Africa: Pentecostal Mega
Churches and a Changing Religious Landscape." Taylor & Francis,
May 29, 2019.
https://www.tandfonline.com/doi/abs/10.1080/17432200.2019
.1590012.

Beliefnet. "Who's Who in Pentecostalism." Beliefnet. Beliefnet
Beliefnet is a lifestyle website providing feature editorial content
around the topics of inspiration, spirituality, health, wellness,
love and family, news and entertainment., June 30, 2016.
https://www.beliefnet.com/faiths/christianity/2006/04/whos-w
ho-in-pentecostalism.aspx.

Bowler, Catherine. "Blessed: A History of the American Prosperity
Gospel." Duke University , 2010.

https://dukespace.lib.duke.edu/dspace/bitstream/handle/1016
1/2297/D_Bowler_Catherine_a_201005.pdf.

Branch, Taylor. *Parting the Waters: America in the King Years, 1954-63*. New York: Simon and Schuster Paperbacks, 2006.

Butler, Stephen M. "The Impact of Advanced Capitalism on Well-Being: An Evidence Based Model." Researchgate, September 14, 2018. https://www.researchgate.net/profile/Stephen_Butler4.

Cadet, Danielle. "Black Church's Civil Rights Movement Legacy Is Both A Blessing And A Curse." HuffPost. HuffPost, August 25, 2013. https://www.huffpost.com/entry/black-church-civil-rights-move ment_n_3810530.

Carroll, Rory, and Jonathan Watts. "Castro's Legacy: How the Revolutionary Inspired and Appalled the World." The Guardian. Guardian News and Media, November 26, 2016. https://www.theguardian.com/world/2016/nov/26/fidel-castro-legacy.

Clinard, Gordon. "Changing Emphases in Contemporary Preaching." Preaching Source. Accessed April 15, 2020. http://preachingsource.com/journal/changing-emphases-in-con temporary-preaching/.

Costello, Thomas. "37 Church Statistics You Need To Know for 2019." *REACHRIGHT*, 25 June 2020, reachrightstudios.com/church-statistics-2019/amp/.

Denning, Steve. "Trump And Authoritarian Propaganda." Forbes. Forbes Magazine, November 15, 2016. https://www.forbes.com/sites/stevedenning/2016/11/06/trump-and-authoritarian-propaganda/#5780d4033e0a.

Desilver, Drew. "US Trails Most Developed Countries In Voter Turnout, ." Factank. Pew Research Center, May 21, 2018. https://www.pewresearch.org/fact-tank/2018/05/21/u-s-voter-turnout-trails-most-developed-countries/.

Economy, Peter. "A New Study of 150,000 Millennials Reveals They Have 10 Surprising Things in Common." Inc.com. Inc., July 27, 2019. https://www.inc.com/peter-economy/a-new-study-of-150000-millennials-revealed-that-they-have-these-10-surprising-things-in-common.html.

Eligon, John. "Where Today's Black Church Leaders Stand on Activism." The New York Times. The New York Times, April 3, 2018. https://www.nytimes.com/2018/04/03/us/mlk-church-civil-rights.html?searchResultPosition=1.

Gaultiere, Bill, Chris, Bill Gaultiere, Bill Gaultiere, Amanda, Bobby, Miriam Knight, et al. "Pastor Stress Statistics." Soul Shepherding, November 20, 2019. https://www.soulshepherding.org/pastors-under-stress/.

Glaeser, Edward L. "How To Talk To Millenials About Capitalism ." *City Journal* . Manhattan Institute of Public Policy, April 2019. https://www.city-journal.org/millennials-embrace-socialism.

Gutierrez, Gustavo. *Theology of Liberation*. Place of publication not identified: Scm Press, 2001.

Jackson, Griffin Paul. "The Top Reasons Young People Drop Out of Church." News & Reporting. Christianity Today, January 16, 2019. https://www.christianitytoday.com/news/2019/january/church-drop-out-college-young-adults-hiatus-lifeway-survey.html.

Jones, Jeffrey M. "U.S. Church Membership Down Sharply in Past Two Decades." Gallup.com. Gallup, April 8, 2020. https://news.gallup.com/poll/248837/church-membership-down-sharply-past-two-decades.aspx.

King, Martin L. Edited by Ali B Ali-Dinar. Letter from a Birmingham Jail [King, Jr.]. University of Pennsylvania . Accessed April 14, 2020. https://www.africa.upenn.edu/Articles_Gen/Letter_Birmingham.html.

Kinnaman, David, and Roxanne Stone. "Americans Divided on the Importance of Church." Barna Group. Barna Group Inc, March 24, 2014. https://www.barna.com/research/americans-divided-on-the-importance-of-church/.

Levy, Joel L. *Time*. Time USA LLC, June 19, 2017. https://time.com/4821911/king-james-bible-history/.

Locke, John. "Second Treatise of Government - Early Modern Texts." Accessed April 14, 2020. http://www.earlymoderntexts.com/assets/pdfs/locke1689a.pdf.

Marcuse, Herbert. *One-Dimensional Man*. London: Routledge, 2002.

Masci, David. "Why Has Pentecostalism Grown so Dramatically in Latin America?" Pew Research Center. Pew Research Center, November 14, 2014. https://www.pewresearch.org/fact-tank/2014/11/14/why-has-pentecostalism-grown-so-dramatically-in-latin-america/.

McEntire, Keshia. "The Church Should Be at the Forefront of the Fight for Social Justice." RELEVANT Magazine, September 12, 2018. https://relevantmagazine.com/current/the-church-should-be-at-the-forefront-of-the-fight-for-social-justice/.

Merker, Matt, and Monique M. Ingalls. "How Contemporary Worship Music Is Shaping Us-for Better or Worse." The Gospel Coalition, February 6, 2019. https://www.thegospelcoalition.org/reviews/singing-congregation-contemporary-worship/.

Meyer, Holly. "What New LifeWay Research Survey Says about Why Young Adults Are Dropping out of Church." The Tennessean. The Tennessean, January 15, 2019. https://www.tennessean.com/story/news/religion/2019/01/15/lifeway-research-survey-says-young-adults-dropping-out-church/2550997002/.

Muller, Peggy, Thomas Costello, Sabrina Addams, Stephen Campbell, Phil Drysdale, Mark Dyar, Elias Torres, and Mel White. "37 Church Statistics You Need To Know for 2019." REACHRIGHT,

January 28, 2020.
https://reachrightstudios.com/church-statistics-2019/.

Neighmond, Patti. "Why A Teen Who Talks Back May Have A Bright
    Future." NPR. NPR, January 3, 2012.
    https://www.npr.org/sections/health-shots/2012/01/03/14449
    5483/why-a-teen-who-talks-back-may-have-a-bright-future.

Newport, Frank. "In U.S., Four in 10 Report Attending Church in Last
    Week." Gallup.com. Gallup, January 6, 2020.
    https://news.gallup.com/poll/166613/four-report-attending-chu
    rch-last-week.aspx.
    Lee, Felicia R. "From Noah's Curse to Slavery's Rationale." *The
    New York Times*, The New York Times, 1 Nov. 2003,
    www.nytimes.com/2003/11/01/arts/from-noah-s-curse-t
    o-slavery-s-rationale.html.

Phil & Co. "Why Millennials Aren't Showing up to Volunteer at Your
    Nonprofit-and How to Get Them There." Phil & Co., January 5,
    2017.
    https://philandcompany.com/how-to-get-millennials-to-volunte
    er/.

"Public Statement by Eight Alabama Clergymen." M.L.King: 1963
    Public statement by 8 Alabama clergymen. Accessed April 14,
    2020.
    https://www.massresistance.org/docs/gen/09a/mlk_day/state
    ment.html.

Reichard , Daniel. "The 1599 Geneva Bible: History's First Study
    Bible." Bible Gateway Blog. Bible Gateway , June 7, 2018.

https://www.biblegateway.com/blog/2017/10/the-1599-geneva
-bible-historys-first-study-bible/.

Roos, Dave. "How Pentecostal Churches Took Over the World."
HowStuffWorks. HowStuffWorks, June 14, 2019.
https://people.howstuffworks.com/pentecostal.htm.

Rousseau , Jean Jacques. "The Social Contract - Early Modern Texts."
Accessed April 14, 2020.
http://www.earlymoderntexts.com/assets/pdfs/rousseau1762.p
df.

Rugani, Kate. "Clergy More Likely to Suffer From Depression,
Anxiety." Duke Today. Duke University , August 27, 2013.
https://today.duke.edu/2013/08/clergydepressionnewsrelease.

Sakuma, Amanda. "The Super-Sized Growth behind Megachurches."
MSNBC. NBCUniversal News Group, October 24, 2014.
http://www.msnbc.com/msnbc/the-super-sized-growth-behind-
megachurches.

Sime, Carley. "Why Toxicity Thrives In The Workplace." Forbes.
Forbes Magazine, February 22, 2019.
https://www.forbes.com/sites/carleysime/2019/02/22/why-toxi
cty-thrives-in-the-workplace/.

Smith, Adam. "Wealth of Nations in PDF for Free." Edited by Mark
Biernat. Political Economy. Political Economy, July 23, 2019.
https://political-economy.com/wealth-of-nations-adam-smith/.

Smith, Bruce Lannes. "Propaganda." Encyclopædia Britannica. Encyclopædia Britannica, inc., March 20, 2020. https://www.britannica.com/topic/propaganda.

Stedman, Ray. "Authentic Christianity." RayStedman.org. Accessed April 14, 2020. https://www.raystedman.org/.

Stockwell, Stephen, and Ruby Jones . "How Hillsong and Other Pentecostal Megachurches Are Redefining Religion in Australia." ABC News. ABC News, September 26, 2019. https://amp-abc-net-au.cdn.ampproject.org/v/s/amp.abc.net.a u/article/11446368?amp_js_v=a3&_gsa=1&usqp=mq331AQFKA GwASA#aoh=15869494901547&csi=1&referrer=https://www.go ogle.com&_tf=From %1$s&share=https://www.abc.net.au/news/2019-08-28/pentec ostal-megachurches-are-redefining-australian-religion/1144636 8.

Stone, Chad, Danilo Trisi, Arloc Sherman, and Jennifer Beltrán. "A Guide to Statistics on Historical Trends in Income Inequality." Center on Budget and Policy Priorities. Center on Budget and Policy Priorities , February 11, 2020. https://www.cbpp.org/research/poverty-and-inequality/a-guide -to-statistics-on-historical-trends-in-income-inequality.

Tamfu, Dieudonné. "The Gods of the Prosperity Gospel: Unmasking American Idols in Africa." Desiring God, April 15, 2020. https://www.desiringgod.org/articles/the-gods-of-the-prosperit y-gospel.

Taub, Amanda. "The Rise of American Authoritarianism." Vox. Vox, March 1, 2016.

https://www.vox.com/2016/3/1/11127424/trump-authoritarianism.

Taylor, Justin. "A Conversation with Four Historians on the Response of White Evangelicals to the Civil Rights Movement." The Gospel Coalition, July 1, 2016. https://www.thegospelcoalition.org/blogs/evangelical-history/a -conversation-with-four-historians-on-the-response-of-white-ev angelicals-to-the-civil-rights-movement/.

The Editors of Encyclopaedia Britannica. "Authoritarianism." Encyclopædia Britannica. Encyclopædia Britannica, inc., November 2, 2017. https://www.britannica.com/topic/authoritarianism.

"The United States Constitution - The U.S. Constitution Online." The United States Constitution - The U.S. Constitution Online - USConstitution.net. Accessed April 14, 2020. https://usconstitution.net/const.html.

Tomasello, Michael. "The Ultra-Social Animal." Wiley Online Library. John Wiley & Sons, Ltd, April 10, 2014. https://onlinelibrary.wiley.com/doi/full/10.1002/ejsp.2015.

Tucker, Carol. "The 1950s – Powerful Years for Religion." USC News. University of Southern California, April 3, 2012. https://news.usc.edu/25835/The-1950s-Powerful-Years-for-Reli gion/. http://www.un.org/en/universal-declaration-human-rights/inde x.html

Wadsworth, Nancy D. "The Racial Demons That Help Explain
Evangelical Support for Trump." *Vox*, Vox, 30 Apr. 2018,
www.vox.com/platform/amp/the-big-idea/2018/4/30/1730128
2/race-evangelicals-trump-support-gerson-atlantic-sexism-segre
gation-south.

White, Edward, and David Widger . "Leviathan, by Thomas Hobbes."
The Project Gutenberg Ebook of Leviathan by Thomas Hobbes,
October 11, 2009.
https://gutenberg.org/files/3207/3207-h/3207-h.htm.